THE HIDDEN VOICE

Also by Lavinia Byrne and published by SPCK

Women Before God (1988)
Sharing the Vision (1989)
The Hidden Tradition (1991)
The Hidden Journey (1993)

THE HIDDEN VOICE

Christian Women and Social Change

EDITED BY

LAVINIA BYRNE

First published in Great Britain 1995
Society for Promoting Christian Knowledge
Holy Trinity Church
Marylebone Road
London NW1 4DU

British Library Cataloguing-in-Publication Data
A catalogue record for this book is available from the British Library

ISBN 0-281-04843-6

Typeset by Wilmaset, Birkenhead, Wirral
Printed in Great Britain by
The Cromwell Press, Melksham, Wiltshire

*This book is dedicated to my colleagues at the
Council of Churches for Britain and Ireland*

CONTENTS

≈

Acknowledgements ix

Introduction 1

1 LET MY LIFE APPEAR 9

2 WILLOW GREEN FOR HOPE UNDONE 23

3 A SURE UNFOLDING 37

4 THE MEDIUM OF THE DIVINE VOICE 50

5 HOUSEHOLD LORE 64

6 A MAGNIFICENT WOMEN'S MEETING 77

7 A HIGH HONOUR AND A PRESSING DUTY 98

8 THIS RELEASE OF WOMEN'S POWER 113

9 BREAKING THE BREAD OF DIVINE KNOWLEDGE 127

10 THE PARADISE OF WOMEN 141

Appendix: Important Dates in the History of the
Women's Suffrage Movement 157

Biographical Notes 165

Bibliography 174

Index 180

I am grateful to the following for permission to reproduce copyright material:

SCM Press for Kathleen Bliss's *The Life and Status of Women in the Churches*; Penguin Books for Rowland Ryder's *Edith Cavell*; The Press and Publications Board of the Church Assembly at Church House, Westminster, for Cecilia Ady's *The Role of Women in the Church*.

Biblical quotations are taken from the *New Revised Standard Version* of the Bible (NRSV) © 1989.

INTRODUCTION

The Hidden Voice is the final volume of a trilogy. Its two elder
sisters are The Hidden Tradition and The Hidden Journey. They
were published in 1991 and 1993 respectively. Each of these
books has taken a strand of women's spiritual writings and offered
their texts for reflection and inspiration in our own times.

When I began collecting and editing material for The Hidden
Tradition, I assumed I would have to impose a shape on what I
discovered in dusty libraries and bookshelves. I had no idea that
the shape of the book would be dictated by the material itself. In
the event I found that the writings of the women whose texts I had
collected imposed this shape on me. I presented the material
without much commentary. After all, each of the extracts served
as a commentary on the others. They fell neatly into eight sections
which told of the writers' experience of God, of the person of
Jesus, of a sense of call, of action and prayer, of endurance and
desire. The final section brought together texts which spoke
about the Virgin Mary.

The Hidden Journey was about the hidden history of the
missionary women. It demonstrated how they believed that they
were bringing a gospel of salvation to those to whom they went as
bearers of the word. In the event, though, they received a
profound sense of liberation themselves. Mary Slessor, the mill
girl from Dundee, became the 'White Queen of the Okoyong';
Gladys Aylward, the parlour maid from Edmonton, became the
'Small Woman' whose exploits in China were celebrated in the
film The Inn of the Sixth Happiness. Each of these women – and
the many like them – discovered that the gospel that they
preached found them out and challenged them to fresh growth.
The book's themes explored the story told in Luke 4.18–19 where
Jesus identified his own mission as a call to 'bring good news to the

poor; to proclaim release to captives and recovery of sight to the blind; to let the oppressed go free; and to proclaim the year of the Lord's favour'.

In the introduction to *The Hidden Journey* I also took up the theme of 'hiddenness'. Why have women's spiritual writings been relegated to the rank of private literature? I noted a twofold conspiracy. First, there is a sense in which women's writings were deemed either trivial or insignificant, or – in the case of mystical writing – even dangerous. Second, women themselves conspired to keep their stories in the private domain, by restricting the reading of letters home from the missionary field. They were shared and discussed in 'Sisterhood' or 'Bright Hour' groups; they were read aloud in the private circle of community recreation in the convents. There was a published literature, but the books were presented in a Sunday-school prize format, as tales of edification and derring-do. The public annals of missionary writing are populated by the stories and voices of the men missionaries.

The present volume starts where the other two left off. It examines the emerging sound of women's voices. It is concerned to study the stories they told. Once again the material imposed the form upon me, for, as I began to examine the sources, I soon discovered a pattern. The sources themselves are interesting, as is this pattern. These are not the gold-embossed Sunday-school prizes. They are not the edifying tales of 'heroines of mercy and daily life' or 'peerless women'. They fall into two main categories which I choose to describe as 'integrated' and 'refused'. In either case they demonstrate a subtle rejection of the contribution of women to the genre. For the integrated literature is writing which has become mainstream. That is to say, if you open any church hymn-book, you will find hymns written by women. Nothing is made of the fact that they were women, that their voices would bring a new sound to the repertoire of Christian hymnody, that they might have a distinctive accent or tone.

The same is true of some of the writings of the women educators. The fact that they wanted education for girls makes them part of a mainstream project, that of Christian education. The literature they generated is not differentiated. It is integrated into the tradition.

But in the case of the women preachers, as with the social purity and suffrage campaigners, something else begins to happen. The story of their apostolic work in the service of the gospel is not integrated into mainstream, orthodox Christian history; it is actively resisted. In this sense, I believe, it is fair to use the word 'refused' to describe this literature. The books tell their own story. Where are they now? Sheila Fletcher's biography of Maude Royden has brought Maude back from the brink of oblivion. But what of Edith Picton-Turberville and Dorothea Hosie? What of the social purity campaigners such as Josephine Butler and Frances Willard, Mary Townsend and Mary Sumner? Organizations such as the Church of England's Mothers' Union or the Josephine Butler Society are proud of their historical roots. But where are the books about these origins? I have some of them in the research library I have collected as a living archive and resource for the threefold 'hidden' project. They are quite extraordinarily hard to come by. And few church libraries or archives hold them in stock.

There is another side to this story of hiddenness. For, as the text will reveal, the social purity and suffrage campaigners were under another threat. Where church historians would write them out of the archives because their secular activities were deemed too radical, secular historians would have a problem with them because they were too religious. So they are betrayed by their brothers, and by the 'sisterhood'.

Sylvia Pankhurst's *The Suffragette Movement* and comparable works have been republished by Virago Press. But their indexes make little of the Christian affiliation of the early suffrage campaigners. You have to search the text to find out that their work for women was motivated by the imperative of the gospel. Millicent Fawcett's life of Josephine Butler was published 'in-house' by the Association for Moral and Social Hygiene. It has not been reprinted.

These brief comments already indicate something about the contents of the book as well as its sources. There are chapters here about the 'lady hymn writers', about the first women preachers, the social purity and suffrage campaigners and the women educators. Chapter 1 examines the emergence of the hidden voice of women through the medium of song. The title, 'Let my Life Appear', comes from the writings of Emily May Grimes. Hers is one of many voices which began to tell out the message of the faith, hope and desire of women during the late-eighteenth and nineteenth centuries. Here we get an intimation of the power, authority and energy which women brought to the task of hymn-writing. We also see that hymn-writing was a direct consequence of literacy. The hymns quoted in this chapter show women at an interface. Here they stand at a place of mediation, between the written and the spoken word, finding a voice that will become a word. What had formerly been hidden as private experience was now to be spoken and sung in the public domain.

Christina Rossetti, one of the most famous of the song-women, supplies the title for Chapter 2. Her line 'Willow green for hope undone' is taken from *Verses*, a collection published by SPCK in 1898. What is distinctive about the sound of her voice and that of the other women hymn-writers? This chapter examines the newly discovered public and theological voice of women. What did they write about? How did they name God? What about the place of the Spirit and the person of Christ? What do we learn about their relationship with their own experience as well as with the Christian mysteries? Above all, is there evidence of a sense of congruence between what they wrote about and the way in which they lived the rest of their lives? As I see it, the voice of the lady hymn-writers was an increasingly liberated as well as liberating one. So we should not be surprised to discover that what had been said in song would also sing in the ministry of the women preachers.

Chapter 3, entitled 'A Sure Unfolding' takes up their story. For when they began to preach women discovered a voice within the Church. This means that the scriptural, theological and social issues which formed their ecclesial context have to be examined. After all, there was resistance to their ministry. Even the true greats such as Catherine Booth, Susannah Wesley, Phoebe Palmer and Maude Royden were opposed. The 'contrary voices' of a hardened opposition spoke out persuasively against the increasing eloquence of women. The words 'A sure unfolding', quoted by Frances Willard, are taken from her book *Woman in the Pulpit*, written in 1888.

As they persevered, the women preachers countered the arguments of the contrary voices, they drew crowds on a scale which is unimaginable nowadays. Helen Bingham, writing about the Irish-Canadian Methodist Ann Preston, supplies the chapter title. Her words about 'The Medium of the Divine Voice' in Ann's prophetic ministry testify to its importance, but also remind us that the utterances of women have sometimes been associated with another medium altogether, that of the dark secrets of oracles and sibyls. The first women preachers had to throw off the myths which would associate their work with 'dark sayings, from of old'. Much of what they said was refreshingly normal; some was more exploratory; some more obviously prophetic. The most prophetic voices prepared the way for the domestic and social campaigners. Their voice would throw down a new challenge to the churches.

The title to Chapter 5 looks innocuous. Yet it was precisely the authority of the experience they had gained attending to 'household lore' which drove the earliest social and purity campaigners towards politics. For in the home the Mary Sumners and Elizabeth Moberly Bells and Frances Willards of this world had learned (at least) three transferable skills. They knew how to cook, how to clean and how to care for others. The language of feminism would talk about nurturing rather than cooking; about networking rather than cleaning; and about health issues rather than caring. But whatever the language, what is important is the insight that in their own homes women gained considerable authority which they would apply in the outer world. That is why Chapter 6 looks at the work of the social campaigners. The words 'A magnificent women's meeting' are taken from Millicent Fawcett's account of a rally organized by Josephine Butler. So what makes a women's meeting magnificent? The energy and sense of purpose which drove the earliest women's organizations explain why so many of them have survived. The YWCA was founded in 1855, the Girls' Friendly Society in 1875, the Mothers' Union in 1876, the Church of Scotland's Woman's Guild in 1887, the Women's World Day of Prayer was founded in the United States in 1890, and the Catholic Women's League in 1906. This hidden history of women's affiliation and mutual support is a fascinating one. In fact, it is hard to remember that once these groups were parodied and hounded because they dared to ask questions about what is good, what is pure and what is healthy. The wisdom acquired in the home now served a more political cause.

Where social campaigning would direct the voices of women towards domestic reality and change their home context, the political work of the suffrage movement was directed towards change at the level of their very identity. The voice which had been heard in the home and then in the world of work, of public morals and of medicine would now empower women in a new way. This was achieved when the sound of politicized women's voices began to be heard. Chapter 7 takes up the story. It has a lofty title. 'A high honour and a pressing duty' were words used by the biographers of Florence Nightingale. She is one of the role models whose history inspired the first suffragettes. For the study of history came as a revelation. The hidden part of the story of women was now examined and explored. Out came Hilda of Whitby as an inspiration to the first educators; out came Joan of Arc for the doughty suffragettes. Role reversal, the possibility of a new identity, was now a distinct possibility. Hence the importance of the Cause.

The Cause was the cause of women's suffrage. How does a nation most publicly endorse the full humanity and identity of its citizens? By giving them the right to vote for their own elected representatives and thereby to direct the public life of the nation. That is why women fought for the vote. That is why the emergence of a fully politicized Christian voice is so integral to the journey into humanity of women. The title of Chapter 8 is taken from the writings of Edith Picton-Turberville. She was witness and participant in this debate because she became a Labour Member of Parliament in 1928. In her book *Christ and Woman's Power* she described enfranchisement as this 'release of women's power' into the world. Such was the experience which is captured for us in the religious testimony of the times. Christ's power and the power of women become identified and equated with the work of the movement.

In the event, however, two world wars followed upon each other with devastating speed. Human nature remained as unredeemed as ever; political life as corrupt. So where did real salvation lie? Where would the voices of women most effectively enact real change? Chapter 9 is called 'Breaking the Bread of Divine Knowledge'. These words are taken from an account by Dorothea Beale of the Cheltenham Ladies' College. They describe her attitude to the sacred ministry of teaching. The women educators brought an educated and trained voice into being. With their work came the possibility of advocacy and education; of a nuanced bid for change. For this reason we should not be surprised that the first educators were so opposed. By offering girls the chance of change, they were disrupting the social order. Hannah More's little village school in Cheddar drew ire from farmers and pastors alike. Once girls were educated, nothing would ever be the same again.

The final chapter examines what the finely tuned voice of the educated woman actually sounded like. Its title, 'The Paradise of Women', is taken from an account of the life of Frances Willard, the educationalist. The hard graft of learning was frequently anything but paradisaical, even when it transformed the lives of a Caroline Hershel or Mary Somerville. Just as the educators had faced opposition, so too did the educated. So what were they to do? Either they could accept the arguments which set up a simple polarization by pitting the scope of women's and men's enter-prises against each other. Or they could go down the more sophisticated route of defending the gospel imperative to preach a liberating word at the risk of changing women's aspirations. In the event this was the route that was chosen. Of course they called for change in women's 'service and status' both within the Church and well beyond its influence as well. Of course they were not prepared to stand still. These were women with 'talents, know-ledge and the power to attract'.

They have their present-day equivalents, as do the women hymn-writers, preachers and social and political campaigners. The 'hidden voice' of women is now a public and authoritative one. It offers a new conversation with the theological, social and political concerns of our own times.

In the work I have done on each of these three volumes of the hidden history of women, I have been helped by my editors at

SPCK. In the case of this third volume, I want to thank Brendan Walsh, who first commissioned it; Philip Law, who saw it through to publication; and the meticulous copy-editor, David Mackinder. There are other people I must thank as well. At the Council of Churches for Britain and Ireland, I want to thank Mary Houston for sharing her time, energy and printer with me. Ruth Burgess from Sunderland collected hymns for me and Janet Wootton helped me locate information about their authors. Diane Atkinson from the Museum of London helped me check out the work of the Christian suffrage groups. The text for the Appendix was kindly supplied by the Pankhurst Centre in Manchester. The staff at the Library of the Fawcett Society helped me identify some of the biographical data. Margaret Joachim of the Fawcett Society offered me inspiration. Enid Castle invited me to preach at the Cheltenham Ladies' College, and Elizabeth Diggory at St Albans Abbey for St Albans High School for Girls. Joy McGibben gave me her own work to read on Josephine Butler. My thanks must also go to Guy J. D. Collins, who has built up a comprehensive database of my thousand-volume library. Information about this resource is now available to any enquirers. There are many, many books to be written about the hidden heritage of Christian women. The present volume does not pretend to be comprehensive; all it offers are some pointers and directions for interpreting the evidence.

Lavinia Byrne IBVM
Feast of the Assumption

CHAPTER 1

~~

LET MY LIFE APPEAR

'Jesus was standing beside the lake of Gennesaret, and the crowd
was pressing in on him to hear the word of God' (Luke 5.1)

*Through the medium and ministry of song, a wide selection of
women began to speak and to write about God with fresh
authority and a new zeal during the eighteenth and especially
the nineteenth centuries. Theirs was a voice that was not
restricted to convent or monastery garden. If anything, it flour-
ished in parsonage and manse. Nor was social class the deter-
mining factor in its emergence. Nuns such as Hildegard of
Bingen and aristocrats such as Elisabeth of Schönau, the twelfth-
century visionary, may have been the pioneers of this tradition.
But theirs was a strangely personal, even a private voice,
whereas the Victorian women who began to make theology in the
public domain through the medium of song adopted a public
voice. Their hymns were to be sung; their words were to be 'told
out'. What does this mean for theological discourse in general, as
well as for questions about women and their making of theology
in particular?*

*This chapter will examine the emergence of women's hymn-
writing as a phenomenon. The next will look at the distinctive
theology of the women who first used this ministry in their
proclamation of the word.*

*Why did women first begin to write hymns which would testify to
the intensity of their faith, hope and desire? The pre-dawn of this
movement is captured here by Lucy A. Bennett, who sets out its
scriptural context.*

Frances R. Havergal

Dear Saviour, thro' the far-spent night
We wait and watch for Thee;
The light of earth for us hath set
Behind dark Calvary.

We yearn to see the rosy dawn
Whose promise gleams afar;
And ever with expectant hearts,
Desire the 'Morning Star'.

Oh Dawn most fair! Oh Day most bright!
Across the Eastern sky
The Advent-glory soon shall break –
'Redemption draweth nigh'.

It may be sooner than we think
Shall end the long delay!
It may be that the Bridegroom-King
E'en now is on His way!

Lucy A. Bennett in Mrs Evan Hopkins, *Hymns of Consecration and Faith* (London: Marshall Brothers Ltd, n.d.), no. 419

There is an amazing sense of expectancy in many of the hymns written by Victorian women. A sense of promise, of something new and better, pervades their texts. But equally there is a constant return to the cross as point of departure, of discovery and of dreams. This is where the true dignity of women was acquired. The words of Elizabeth Jane Clephane, 'Beneath the cross of Jesus, I fain would take my stand,' supply a clue. A dialogue is initiated when women first begin to sing aloud to God. This dialogue is one which is deeply devotional, but equally it is one which empowers the singer. She is not to be cast down or burdened under the grief of her Saviour or beneath the weight of any personal guilt. Like Jesus at the sea of Gennesaret, she is to stand upright where she is most truly known and to derive life and energy from this stance.

Fanny Crosby, the North American author of 9,000 hymns, who died at the age of ninety-five, writes one of the most famous of these sacred songs.

Blessed assurance – Jesus is mine!
Oh, what a foretaste of glory divine!
Heir of salvation, purchase of God;
Born of his Spirit, washed in his blood.

CHORUS: This is my story, this is my song,
Praising my Saviour all the day long;
This is my story, this is my song,
Praising my Saviour all the day long.

Perfect submission, perfect delight,
Visions of rapture burst on my sight;

Angels descending, bring from above
Echoes of mercy, whispers of love.

Perfect Submission, all is at rest,
I in my Saviour am happy and blest;
Watching and waiting, looking above,
Filled with his goodness, lost in his love.

Redemption Hymnal (Eastbourne: Victory Press, 1951), no. 370

The word 'author' is used carefully of Fanny Crosby because – in spite of her powerful visual imagery, especially in the second verse – she was in fact blind from birth and dictated all her work. In this sense she was not a writer, because the only thing she ever wrote was her own signature. In this sense too, she is a powerful symbol of the woman who stands at the interface of the spoken and the written word and who converts the one into the other. This, in essence, is what the 'lady hymn writers' did. The title was given to them by their biographer, Mrs E. R. Pitman, in 1892. Her 369-page study covered the Catholic end of the tradition, or – as she put it – 'Hymn Writers for the Sanctuary', 'Minor Hymn Writers: English' (where the Welshwoman Ann Griffiths figures prominently) and 'Minor Hymn Writers: American'. There then follow chapters on 'Hymn Writers for the Quiet Hour', 'Hymn Writers who were also Poetesses', 'Writers of Children's Hymns' and 'Queenly and Noble Hymn Writers'. Her text is largely narrative and descriptive rather than discursive. The nearest she comes to analysis is in her introduction, where she notes:

One thing more. It will be noticed in these chronicles that God's singers have come from all ranks and conditions of life, as well as from all branches of the Church militant. Some have worn queenly crowns, others have toiled for a daily living; some have been nursed in the lap of wealth among the aristocracy, others have filled very humble positions in life; some have rejoiced in health and vigour, others have been lifelong invalids; some have adhered to orthodox and fashionable church systems, others have clung to unorthodox faiths, and to the chilling shadows of dissent. Yet in one and all we can trace the family likeness.

Mrs E. R. Pitman, *Lady Hymn Writers*
(London: T. Nelson & Sons, 1892), p. 19

This likeness is the fact that these are all women. Half Hours with the Hymn Book, *a commentary on the 1904* Hymn Book *of the Methodist Church, published by Charles H. Kelley and written by Mary Champness, gives further notes on some forty-one women hymn-writers. The names on her list read like a litany of the great and the good. She plunges straight into her text with Mrs Alexander, the author of 'Once in Royal David's City', and emerges eight pages later with Anna Letitia Waring, who wrote 'My heart is resting', based on Lamentations 3.24. Mary Champness comments: 'Not many hymns have been based on texts from this book, and certainly very few have this ring of happy trust about them,' adding, 'Miss Waring's hymns are in the major key, not like Miss Procter's.' It transpires that Miss Procter's offence was that she was a Roman Catholic, 'which may partly account for the plaintive tendency of her hymns'. For 'the bringing up of a Romanist does not tend to the making of good and singable sacred poetry'. So much for the insouciant inclusivity of Mrs Pitman's family likeness!*

Among the authors she praises by name is Frances Ridley Havergal. Like Fanny Crosby, Havergal is one of the great voices of the period. In her book The Ministry of Song, *she identified the cosmic and public dimensions of her sense of purpose and call:*

> 'What wouldst thou be?'
> The question hath wakened wild thoughts in me,
> And a thousand responses, like ghosts from their graves,
> Arise from my soul's unexplored deep caves,
> The echoes of every varying mood
> Of a wayward spirit all unsubdued;
> The voices which thrill through my inmost breast
> May tell me of gladness, but not of rest.

What wouldst thou be?
'T is well that the answer is not for me.

'What wouldst thou be?'
An eagle soaring rejoicingly.
One who may rise on the lightning's wing,
Till our wide, wide world seem a tiny thing;
Who may stand on the confines of boundless space,
And the giant form of the universe trace,
While its full grand harmonies swell around,
And grasp it all with mind profound.
Such would I be,
Only stayed by infinity.

Frances Ridley Havergal, *The Ministry of Song*
(London: James Nisbet & Co., 1885), pp. 54–5

The sense of glory and empowerment is repeated. Here we have an intimation of what the experience of salvation should mean for women. And here too we are presented with a theological text which testifies to a high degree of literacy. Now, are we to treat this as a marvel, and thereby to turn the women who wrote hymns into an array of freaks? With Doctor Johnson, are we to imply that it is astonishing 'that they do it at all'? Or are we to accept the line adopted by Emma Pitman?

Hymnody is attracting much notice at the present time, but only a student of the subject can realize how much we owe to lady hymn writers. It takes poetic feeling, fervent devotion, and religious experience to make a good hymn, and all these must be conceded to most of our women hymn writers, as we think the specimens here given will prove.

Mrs E. R. Pitman, *Lady Hymn Writers*
(London: T. Nelson & Sons, 1892), p. 1

This borders on the coy in its claims for what makes a good hymn and for what it is natural for women to bring to the craft of hymn-

writing. In our own times we might argue that a good hymn is one which has a serious theological purpose, or one which offers praise to God, or one with a good tune. A study such as this one, however, would also want to search the texts for evidence that women did more than have poetic feelings and fervent devotion. After all, men can have those in good measure as well. The gender stereotyping of human feelings does little to uncover what is distinctive about the hymn-writing of women.

Another commentator on hymnody, Erik Routley, writing in 1952, grapples with this question in his chapter on 'Women Hymn-Writers'.

The reader will not fail to observe in this and the three foregoing chapters a tacit acceptance of the ancient classification of human beings into men, women and clergymen. It is possible, also, that the reader will feel less objection to the segregation of the clergy than to that of the women in this connection. It is one of the marks of the twentieth century that many attributes which had been regarded as feminine properties were found, or at least asserted, to be accidents of the feminine state, and the separation of these accidents has brought with it a reaction against the sharp cleavage between the sexes which was one of the marks of Victorian England.

Now it happens that women have made a contribution to hymnody parallel to that which they have made to English letters. But there is one curious difference between the two contributions, which is that while the emancipation of women has produced a substantial increase in the number, and an enormous elevation of the literary standard, of women novelists, the coming of that age corresponds exactly with a virtual drying-up of the gift of hymn-writing in women.

Erik Routley, *Hymns and Human Life*
(London: John Murray, 1952), p. 203

All this is a long way away from the assumptions of Mrs Pitman a century earlier. Whether or not one agrees with Dr Routley's claim that women are no longer writing decent hymns, his assertion

15

certainly moves the argument to a new place. The phenomenon is not that women wrote hymns; what is astonishing is that they wrote them in such abundance at a particular time in history.

So what was significant about the late-eighteenth and nine-teenth centuries? Two answers emerge. One is about women and literacy, meaning the ability to write things down. Fanny Crosby's blindness has already been referred to as an explanation of why she did not write out her own hymns. Ann Griffiths' story is taken up by Emma Pitman.

It is remarkable that she scarcely ever *wrote* her hymns, and had it not been for the faithful memory of a servant in her home, they would have been quite lost. To this woman – named Ruth – Ann Griffiths used to repeat her hymns as soon as composed; and then the two women would sing them over to hymns tunes until they had learned them. After the hymnist's death, Ruth repeated these hymns to her husband, who wrote them from her dictation. We quote one hymn which seems too good to be passed by, but there are many others of the same high character:

> Must I face the stormy river?
> There is One to break its flood –
> Christ, my great High-priest and faithful,
> Christ, my all-sufficient good.
> Through his blood shall come the triumph
> Over death and hell to me;
> And I shall be, in his likeness,
> Sinless through eternity.
>
> Disembodied of all evil,
> I shall pierce with earnest eyes
> Into Calvary's deep wonders,
> And its infinite surprise;
> The Invisible beholding,
> Who is living, and was dead,
> In a pure unbroken union
> With the ever-living Head.

There I shall exalt the Person,
God's own Sacrifice divine,
Without any veil or fancy –
And my soul like him shall shine.
With the mystery revealed
In his wounds, I shall commune;
Losing sight no more for ever
Of the all-beloved Son.

From salvation's highest fountains,
Oh, to drink with each new day!
Till my thirst for earthly pleasures
Has completely passed away.
Walking always for my Master,
Quick to answer to his call;
Then to hold the door wide open,
And enjoy him, all in all.

Ann Griffiths in Mrs E. R. Pitman, Lady Hymn Writers
(London: T. Nelson & Sons, 1892), pp. 174–5

In the event, Ann Griffiths had to face the stormy river sooner than she anticipated. She died at the age of twenty-nine, after a short married life of about ten months. Of Ruth – and her phenomenal memory – Mrs Pitman tells us nothing further. Yet the tableau of these interweaving lives is a fascinating one. And made additionally so by the fact that Ann originally composed her hymns in Welsh. Here we have a society poised on the brink of literacy. And women stand at the intersection, finding a voice which will become a word.

The huge hunger of Ann Griffiths' enjoyment of God makes for an extraordinary role reversal. It is she who comes with desire, questing for her divine Lover. He meanwhile loiters among the myrtles, a Rose of Sharon with a white and red complexion.

Lo, between the myrtles standing,
One who merits well my love,

Though his worth I guess but dimly
High all earthly things above;
Happy morning
When at last I see him clear!

Rose of Sharon, so men name Him;
White and red His cheeks adorn;
Store untold of Earthly treasure
Will His merit put to scorn;
Friend of sinners,
He their pilot o'er the deep.

What can weigh with me henceforth
All the idols of the earth?
One and all I here proclaim them,
Matched with Jesus, nothing worth;
O to rest me
All my lifetime in His love!

Ann Griffiths, translated from the Welsh by Sir H. Idris Bell

'Is there a scholarship that grows / naturally as the lichen?' R. S. Thomas would ask in his 'Fugue for Ann Griffiths', forgetting perhaps that the principal influence on her was the chapel where she learned her Calvinism. Her mysticism leads her to use the language of desire, but the vocabulary is deeply scriptural. Zechariah's myrtles and Isaiah's roses are garlanded together in a series of allusions which remind us of the extraordinary power of memory in the mind of someone who could not write. But what led Ann and the other women who composed in their heads to pour out their testimony in this way?

There seems to be a clear answer to this question, and it forms a second theme in the emergence of women's voices. The Word sought out Ann Griffiths' voice because in this way she could testify to the saving work of redemption. She was saved and could tell other people what this meant to her in an exchange where mutuality was the key. In this sense a personal experience becomes the medium of public grace, and what is awesome in these testimonies is the authority with which the women hymn-writers use the word 'I'. This hymn by Annie Marston is a case in point.

I thank Thee, Lord, that Thou hast shown,
And I begin to see,
What Thou canst be to all Thine own;
What they may be to Thee,
If only they will yield Thee all,
And trustingly obey Thy call.

How wonderful! I never knew
That I might trust Thee so;
That Thou wouldst be so much to me,
In all the way I go,
That ev'ry need Thou wouldst supply,
And all my longings satisfy.

I take Thee as my Keeper now,
And I commit to Thee
My soul, my way, my works, my cause,
In Thy sole charge to be;
And my deposit, Thou, I know,
Wilt guard secure from ev'ry foe.

I take Thee for my Peace, O Lord,
My heart to keep and fill,
Thine own great calm amid earth's storms
Shall keep me always still.
And as Thy kingdom doth increase,
So shall Thine ever-deepening peace.

I take Thee as my Wisdom too,
For wisdom's sum Thou art;
Thou, who dost choose the foolish things,
Set me henceforth apart,

That I may speak and work for Thee
And Thou shalt work and speak in me.

I take Thee, Lord, to be my All,
Since all Thou art is mine,
I nothing have, and nothing am;
That nothing, Lord, is thine.
Thou shalt be everything to me,
In all things my sufficiency.

Annie Marston in Mrs Evan Hopkins, *Hymns of Consecration
and Faith* (London: Marshall Brothers Ltd, n.d.), no. 472

*In reading this hymn, it helps to be reminded that the British
Married Women's Property Act – which allowed women the right
to own property and also to keep some of their earnings – came into
force only in 1882. The God who is Keeper, Peace, Wisdom and
Lord to Annie Marston is a God with whom she could discuss
transactions and deposits, supply and satisfaction before any
woman could do so with her husband. In such a climate, it is
normal that hymn-writing should engage with the quest for
freedom represented by legislation about women and property –
even if it does so quite unconsciously. Here the sense that 'Advent-
glory', or expectancy, was about redemption is fleshed out in the
lived experience of women who were struggling to begin to
understand what the meaning of salvation might be in their own
context. To say this is not to attribute the insights of liberation
theology a generation before their time. It is simply to notice that
when women stand at some kind of interface, as they did here
when they sought to know and communicate the Word, then
something begins to happen which has a profoundly transforming
effect. That is why there is more to this text than meets the eye. In
verse five, Annie prays to be set apart for ministry: 'That I may
speak and work for Thee, / And Thou shalt work and speak in me.'
Speaking – or discovering a hidden voice – is irreducibly linked to
work or to doing. This means moving from the private to the public
sphere.*

Others would write in the same vein, among them Emily May Grimes.

Speak Lord in the stillness,
While I wait on Thee;
Hush'd my heart to listen,
In expectancy.

Speak, O blessèd Master,
In this quiet hour;
Let me see Thy face, Lord,
Feel Thy touch of power.

For the words Thou speakest,
They are life indeed;
Living bread from heaven,
Now my spirit feed!

All to Thee is yielded,
I am not my own;
Blissful, glad surrender,
I am Thine alone.

Speak, Thy servant heareth,
Be not silent, Lord;
Waits my soul upon Thee
For the quickening word.

Fill me with the knowledge
Of Thy glorious will;
All Thine own good pleasure
In Thy child fulfil.

Like a watered garden
Full of fragrance rare,
Lingering in Thy presence
Let my life appear.

Emily May Grimes in Trustees of the Keswick Convention, *The Keswick Hymn-Book* (London: Marshall, Morgan & Scott Ltd, n.d.), p. 6

This time the text uses New Testament imagery, from the Advent expectancy of the first verse, through the 'touch of power' of the second, to the consummation of heavenly presence in the new garden of the resurrection. The word is here portrayed as a quickening or life-giving word and is identified with knowledge and pleasure.

The constant themes are of relationship and of communication. Of a Word who is spoken into the hearts of women so that they should impart him to others, now with the wisdom of the Scriptures, now through the accents of the great themes of salvation. If anything, what most characterizes the emerging voice of the women hymn-writers is the certainty that what was formerly spoken should now be written; what was formerly private should now become public; what formerly lingered should now appear. But what was the specific sound of this new theological voice as it became so richly articulated and increasingly public? This is what the next chapter must now explore.

CHAPTER 2

~

WILLOW GREEN FOR HOPE UNDONE

'Then the prophet Miriam, Aaron's sister, took a tambourine in her hand;
and all the women went out after her with tambourines and with dancing.
And Miriam sang to them . . .' (Exodus 15.20–1)

> While Christ lay dead the widowed world
> Wore willow green for hope undone:
> Till, when bright Easter dews impearled
> The chilly burial earth,
> All north and south, all east and west,
> Flushed rosy in the arising sun;
> Hope laughed, and Faith resumed her rest,
> And Love remembered mirth.

Christina Rossetti, *Verses* (London: SPCK, 1898), p. 75

Christina Rossetti's poem is entitled 'Our Church Palms are Budding Willow Twigs'. In 1874, another woman song-writer, Sarah Geraldine Stock, had composed 'Lord, Thy ransomed Church is waking' for the London February Mission.

> Lord, Thy ransomed Church is waking
> Out of slumber far and near,
> Knowing that the morn is breaking
> When the Bridegroom shall appear;
> Waking up to claim the treasure
> With Thy precious life-blood bought,
> And to trust in fuller measure
> All Thy wondrous death hath wrought.

Original illustration from 'Uncle Tom's Cabin'

'Little Eva reading the Bible to Uncle Tom.'

'To her class of school-children she [Mrs. Stowe] read her first description of the most saintly child in American literature.'

Praise to Thee for this glad shower,
Precious drops of latter rain,
Praise that by Thy Spirit's power
Thou hast quickened us again;
That Thy Gospel's priceless treasure,
Now is borne from land to land,
And that all the Father's pleasure
Prospers from Thy piercèd hand.

Praise to Thee for saved ones yearning
O'er the lost and wandering throng;
Praise for voices daily learning
To upraise the glad new song;
Praise to Thee for sick ones hasting
Now to touch Thy garment's hem;
Praise for souls believing – tasting
All Thy love has won for them.

Set on fire our heart's devotion
With the love of Thy dear name;
Till o'er every land and ocean
Lips and lives Thy cross proclaim.
For our eyes on Thy returning,
Keeping watch till Thou shalt come,
Loins well girt, lamps brightly burning,
Then Lord, take Thy servants home.

Sarah Geraldine Stock in Mrs Evan Hopkins, *Hymns of Consecration
and Faith* (London: Marshall Brothers Ltd, n.d.), no. 429

Of Christina Rossetti, Miss Champness could write that she was

. . . a far greater poetess than any we have yet named, a sister of
Rossetti the poet and painter; but her life was never marred by the
sad lapses into vice and sensuality that some would have us believe
are a necessary evil to those born with the artistic temperament.

Mary Champness, *Half Hours with the Hymn Book*
(London: Charles H. Kelley, n.d.), pp. 260–1

Contemporary dictionaries of biography are somewhat blunter, and attribute the ill-health she enjoyed for most of her life to psychosomatic causes. Whatever the truth, there is a world of difference between the High Anglican devotion she espoused and the robust evangelical piety of Sarah Stock. Socially they were divided too, so that records of Rossetti are everywhere, whereas Miss Stock has vanished from all but the oldest hymn-books and is barely recorded in the histories.

But the parallels, even with random samples such at these, are striking evidence of what Mrs Pitman called 'family likeness'. For both authors lean towards the same scriptural and dogmatic sources, despite their different ecclesial backgrounds. They are concerned with the meaning of 'life out of death' as interpreted through the resurrection of Jesus. Yet – and this is where something distinctive is revealed – both draw out their theological message in language and metaphors which look innocent enough, but which presage the dialogue which feminism claims to have initiated.

So what are the parallels between them, and what is the distinctive note in these women's teaching? Both write sacred songs about the Church as a universal community, spread 'far and near' to every point of the compass. The Church is a community of the redeemed, a 'ransomed Church', 'flushed rosy in the arising sun'. Both write Christological hymns whose focus is the 'bright Easter' whose 'morn is breaking'. Both seek to quicken hope, faith and love. In this sense the parallels are evident.

'While Christ lay dead the widowed world / Wore willow green'. Now it is feminism which has taught us to use such words as 'women's experience' and to turn to the Scriptures for an insight into the relationship Jesus had with women. Yet here are the foremothers, in their quaint Victorian language, doing precisely that. The widowed world was that of the women who had stood at the foot of the cross and then buried the body of Jesus to await anointing after the Sabbath. It was the widowed world which welcomed the 'glad shower' of redemption as a touch of the garment of Jesus. Our own world is fascinated by cosmology; Victorian women wrote about the earth as a place of divine visitation. While Rossetti is cool and detached about this, Stock

waits for the bridegroom with eager longing, her 'loins well girt, lamps brightly burning'.

And lest these be perceived as isolated instances of a distinctive women's voice, there are two other theological themes which can be pursued through the sacred songs of the period. The first is about the 'voices daily learning' of which Sarah Stock wrote; the second is about the way in which God is named in the hymns of the women writers. These themes come together in a piece by the eighteenth-century Baptist, Anne Steele.

Father of mercies, in Thy word
What endless glory shines!
For ever be Thy name adored
For these celestial lines.

Here springs of consolation rise
To cheer the fainting mind,
And thirsty souls receive supplies,
And sweet refreshment find.

Here the Redeemer's welcome voice
Spreads heavenly peace around;
And life and everlasting joys
Attend the blissful sound.

Oh, may these hallowed pages be
My ever dear delight!
And still new beauties may I see,
And still increasing light.

Divine Instructor, gracious Lord,
Be Thou for ever near;
Teach me to love Thy sacred word,
And view my Saviour here.

Anne Steele in Charles Vincent and D. J. Wood,
The Hymnal Companion to the Book of Common Prayer
(London: Longmans, Green & Co., 1922), no. 268

This exultant song of praise to literacy is written as a commentary on Jeremiah 15.16, 'thy word was unto me the joy and rejoicing of mine heart'. Anne Steele calls God 'Father of mercies', a name crafted from her own experience and memories. Her own father was a timber merchant, the pastor of Broughton Parish Church in Hampshire. Her fiancé Mr Elscourt had been drowned in the River Avon just as they were about to be married. We do not know who taught her to read. All we do know is that she turns to God with a kind of lyricism as her 'Divine Instructor' as she opens the Scriptures in the certainty that they will show her 'still new beauties'. So, ringing around in her song is the insight that God speaks and that she may hear and learn the divine word, so that thirsty souls may 'receive supplies'. There is a nascent apostolic yearning in what she seeks to understand.

Among the thirsty souls were those for whom Lucy A. Bennett wrote the hymn, 'For an Opening Meeting'. It provides a trinitarian formula of considerable interest (in verse two) as well as an early example of the feel of women's preaching. Lucy Bennett asked people what they thought; she hunted out the core nature of their belief and rounded on them with all the ferocity of a John the Baptist. In the last verse, her hymn offers an engaging theology of community.

What think ye? Has the Living Head
His presence e'er denied?
What think ye? Shall the feast be spread,
And not the host preside?

What think ye? That He will not do
As He hath ever done?
Our First, our Last, our Centre too,
Blessed Father, Spirit, Son.

What think ye? That He will not stand
Amid the shadows dim
To welcome with extended hand
All who keep trust with Him?

Away with all unworthy thoughts!
Prepare the way! Prepare!
Jehovah Shammah thou hast sought?
Be glad. The Lord is here!

Seek audience with the Lord of Love,
Expect, His face to see,
And this in very truth shall prove
A Peniel to thee.

Let faith extend her mantle wide,
Enlarging her request,
So shall his heart be satisfied,
Who loves to give the best.

Forecast His blessed work of grace,
Make straight His paths! Prepare!
Low in the very dust Thy place,
We reach high blessing there.

What think ye? Lord, our thoughts would be
Lofty and just and true: —
Expectant, as we wait to see
Thy wonders old and new.

Thyself all loyal hearts confess
Incomparably dear;
Yet closer to each other press
Because to Thee so near.

Lucy A. Bennett in Mrs Evan Hopkins, *Hymns of Consecration
and Faith* (London: Marshall Brothers Ltd, n.d.), no. 558

*'Our thoughts would be / Lofty and just and true'. What value
should we attribute to this exalted rhetoric? Is there any sense in
which these are easy words? Or do they reveal another theme in*

the women hymn-writers' work which can be characterized and analysed still further? When Christian women begin to write hymns, are they laying out the ground rules for social and political change? If this is true of the hymns given here, is it true of some of the more familiar texts which are given in the classic hymn-books? Can they be read as critically as those examined here?

This is dangerous territory, for historians have been careful to remind us that we cannot simply reread texts from our own perspective and put our own thoughts and concerns into what we find there. A critical analysis must bear this insight in mind. What we do find when we examine the evidence is a kind of congruence between what the women wrote about and what they did in the rest of their lives. Julia Ward Howe, the author of 'Mine eyes have seen the glory of the coming of the Lord', was an ardent campaigner for female suffrage and for the abolition of slavery. Harriet Beecher Stowe campaigned against slavery. Her Uncle Tom's Cabin *was published in 1851. These are perhaps extreme examples. The story is taken up by Lady McDougall, the author of* Songs of the Church, *in her chapter on Mrs Cecil Frances Alexander.*

In 1850 she married William Alexander, afterwards Bishop of Derry and Raphoe, and now Archbishop of Armagh. At the time of their marriage he was rector of a wide country parish in County Tyrone, where the population was scattered over miles of mountains and bogs. Here Mrs Alexander arrived as a bride, and here, during five years, she got through a vast amount of work.

In those days district nurses were unknown, parish doctors were scarce, yet poverty and sickness had to be met. Day after day, in that remote parish, Mrs Alexander might be seen crossing the wet moorland in all weathers, carrying nourishing food, or warm clothing, or medical comforts, to the poor and helpless.

One day she found a poor paralysed woman shivering with cold, for the bedclothes were scanty; and, unwilling to leave her thus, Mrs Alexander took off her outer wrap, and folded it round the limbs of the poor sufferer.

In another cottage she found a woman in great pain from a bad wound, untended and altogether without medical aid. For six weeks every day Mrs Alexander came to this woman, and herself washed and dressed the wound, until healing set in and she recovered her health.

No severe weather, or long distance, or the demands of society were allowed to interfere with these duties to the helpless and suffering.

In this parish her eldest child was born, and here, in happy hours of leisure, she wrote some of her finest poems . . .

As life went on, and she came into contact with all sorts and conditions of men, her sympathies widened, and she was drawn to all who loved righteousness, whether within or without the pale of the Church. For she was getting ready to join the great multitude which no man can number, clothed in white raiment. After forty-five years of loving work in the north of Ireland, she went to her rest.

At her funeral crowds of people, English, Irish, Catholics, and Protestants, mingled their tears; for all loved her, and felt that a saint had gone from their midst.

Lady Ellen M. McDougall, *Songs of the Church with Stories of their Writers* (London: Charles H. Kelly, n.d.), pp. 278–82

Practical charity and a growing love for righteousness are here identified as the marks of Mrs Alexander's life. The language may have dated, but the instinct is sound. For Lady McDougall here presents Mrs Alexander within a dense net of relationships. They form her context and supply her with her imagery. The green hill of her most famous composition, for instance, was a little grass-covered hill outside Derry which she passed daily in her carriage when on her way to the shops. One of her hymns, an early study in inclusive language, is passionate in the synthesis it makes. Power, peace, strength and love stand alongside each other as the gifts of the Spirit and an aid to discernment, or right leading.

Spirit of God, that moved of old
Upon the waters' darkened face,
Come, when our faithless hearts are cold,
And stir them with an inward grace.

Thou that art power and peace combined,
All highest strength, all purest love,
The rushing of the mighty wind,
The brooding of the gentle dove,

Come, give us still thy powerful aid,
And urge us on and keep us thine;
Nor leave the hearts that once were made
Fit temples for thy grace divine.

Nor let us quench thy sevenfold light;
But still with softest breathings stir
Our wayward souls and lead us right,
O Holy Ghost, the Comforter.

Mrs Alexander in *Church Praise*
(London: James Nisbet & Co. Ltd, 1907), no. 168

Once again, this is not an isolated example. Mrs Fry, too, is singled out by the commentators.

Mrs Elizabeth Fry, a member of the Society of Friends, and known to fame the whole world over as the 'Quaker philanthropist', tried her hand at the composition of hymns. Seeing, however, that Quakers do not *sing* in their meetings, and possess no hymnbook, it is only fair to suppose that she intended her hymns for reading only, as a means of private devotion. The one which we shall quote has crept into several hymnbooks, and has become a great favourite with devout and intelligent readers.

For what shall I praise thee, my God and my King,
For what blessings the tribute of gratitude bring?
Shall I praise thee for pleasure, for health, and for ease,
For the spring of delight, and the sunshine of peace?

Shall I praise thee for flowers that bloomed on my breast,
For joys in perspective, and pleasures possessed,
For the spirits that brightened my days of delight,
For the slumbers that sat on my pillow at night?

For this I would praise thee; but if only for this,
I should leave half untold the donation of bliss;
I thank thee for sickness, for sorrow, for care,
For the thorns I hath gathered, the anguish I bear.

For nights of anxiety, watching, and tears –
A present of pain, a perspective of fears;
I praise thee, I bless thee, my King and my God,
For the good and the evil thy hand hath bestowed.

The flowers were sweet, but their fragrance is flown;
They yielded no fruits, they are withered and gone:
The thorn it was poignant, but precious to me,
'Twas the message of mercy – it led me to thee!

Although Mrs Fry's life and career are known to the majority of readers, it may not be amiss to give a slight sketch of them. She was a Gurney by birth, and was born in Norwich in 1780. The celebrated Friend, Joseph John Gurney, was her elder brother. From youth she was remarkable for her benevolent aspirations and efforts, and before her marriage established a school for eighty poor children in the large kitchen of her father's house. After her marriage she continued and increased, with the consent of her husband, her disinterested philanthropic labours. Quite accidentally one day Mrs Fry visited Newgate, and from this visit her efforts for the amelioration of the conditions of prisoners arose. Her visits were repeated, and, in spite of the remonstrances of the jailer and turnkeys, she insisted on remaining alone in the midst of one hundred and sixty women, who were more like wild beasts than anything else. They listened in silent astonishment at first, but the astonishment soon gave way to respect and affection. Mrs Fry was besought to repeat her visit, which she did, and passed a whole day with them, reading the Bible, talking with them, and hearing their tales of sorrow and of sin. By degrees she won their confidence, set up a school for them, gave them employment, made rules for their guidance, and appointed one of their number as superintendent of the rest. As they left the prison on the completion of their sentences she befriended these outcasts, and either restored them to their homes or obtained situations for them. Afterwards she travelled through England, Scotland, and Ireland, as well as through Continental countries, seeking to assuage and improve the condition of prisoners, lunatics, and similar helpless members of the population. She was not less active in works of goodness near home; and though visited by much affliction at times, until she passed away, at the age of sixty-five, she was honoured by kings, queens, and emperors, beloved by all Christians of whatever sect, and regretted by the poor and needy. She cared nothing for fame, but she found fame of the most enduring kind.

Mrs E. R. Pitman, *Lady Hymn Writers*
(London: T. Nelson & Sons, 1892), pp. 181–3

Mrs Fry's hymn speaks of 'the message of mercy' which she received from 'nights of anxiety, watching, and tears'. 'The donation of bliss' is measured out for her in sickness, sorrow and care. The school in which she put herself to learn was that of 'disinterested philanthropic labours'. In the event, however, she became a radical opponent of current practice and an ardent campaigner for change. Her voice became the voice of the soul of the nation because her authority was gained by working with prisoners at Newgate and women on the convict ships. She translated praxis into words of passion and power.

The present-day reader of the earliest women hymn-writers' work has an interesting task. Do we read these sacred songs as though they were anodyne? As though the struggle they describe is an internal one, with the forces of good and evil somehow warring away quietly inside a genteel heart? Or do we allow them to sing with some of the power of the women who first wrote them? The conspiracy which has kept these women hidden is a persuasive one. Yet their fresh theology and forceful language open up a new vein of communication at the heart of the Church's proclamation of the word. As Emily May Grimes knew, theirs was a liberated and a liberating voice.

The Master comes! He calls for thee –
Go forth at His almighty word;
Obedient to His last command;
And tell to those who never heard,
Who sit in deepest shades of night,
That Christ has come to give them light!

The Master calls! Arise and go:
How blest His messenger to be!
He who has given thee liberty,
Now bids thee set the captives free;
Proclaim His mighty power to save,
Who for the world his life-blood gave.

The Master calls! Shall not thy heart
In warm responsive love reply,
'Lord, here am I, send me, send me –
Thy willing slave – to live or die:
An instrument unfit indeed,
Yet Thou wilt give me what I need.'

And if thou canst not go, yet bring
An offering of a willing heart;
Then, though thou tarriest at home,
Thy God shall give thee too thy part.
The messengers of peace upbear
In ceaseless and prevailing prayer.

Short is the time for service true,
For soon shall dawn that glorious day
When, all the harvest gathered in,
Each faithful heart shall hear Him say,
'My child, well done! your toil is o'er;
Enter My joy for evermore.'

Emily May Grimes in

Trustees of the Keswick Convention, *The Keswick Hymn-Book*
(London: Marshall, Morgan & Scott Ltd, n.d.), no. 408

It was no coincidence that Emily May Grimes made the final connection: the women hymn-writers discovered a voice that would propel women 'to preach the resurrection of the Lord!' What had been said in song would sing in the spoken word.

'With one accord' within an upper room
The faithful followers of Jesus met:
One was the hope of every waiting soul,
And on one object great each heart was set.

'With one accord,' until the mighty gift
Of pentecostal power was outpoured;
Then forth as witnesses possessed of God,
To preach the resurrection of the Lord!

'With one accord' within the house of God
A hallelujah song is daily raised,
As with the voice of one, from vocal hearts
Jehovah's name is glorified and praised.

Pour down Thy Spirit once again, dear Lord;
Our cry goes up to Thee for 'latter rain';
Unite Thy people as the 'heart of one,'
And pentecostal days shall come again!

Emily May Grimes in Trustees of the Keswick Convention, *The Keswick Hymn-Book* (London: Marshall, Morgan & Scott Ltd, n.d.), no. 150

CHAPTER 3

~

A SURE UNFOLDING

'My words that I have put in your mouth shall not depart out of
your mouth' (Isaiah 59.21)

Frances Willard's Woman in the Pulpit *was published in 1888.
In it she writes, 'Let us now hear from a few "women
preachers" ', and goes on to list testimonies from a broadly based
collection of the five hundred women in the United States who
'have already entered the pulpit as evangelists'. These testimonies are exultant and defensive by turns. Some argue passionately, others are more moderate. All are confident that the work
they do is God's work.*

A leading Quaker preacheress and editor writes as follows:—
'The prophecy of Joel ii.28–30 settles the question for our
dispensation, and the Apostolic Church recognizes this liberty
and the call to prophesy, and allowed it in so far as the prejudices
and customs of that Oriental country would permit. I think the
equality of men and women under the Gospel was one of the great
principles that was to be announced by the apostles, and then left
to a sure unfolding.

The truth is, every revolution of the wheel of evangelization
brings this truth into fuller recognition. It is very interesting to
me to see how God is providentially making room for us, in spite
of the iron-clad prejudices of the churches.'

Frances E. Willard, *Woman in the Pulpit*
(Boston: D. Lothrop Co., 1888), pp. 100–1

Mrs. Booth at the Dome, Brighton

Mrs Phoebe Palmer, the Revivalist preacher, also turns to the authority of the Scriptures and of tradition to establish the context for her call to speak.

The Scriptural idea of the terms preach and prophesy stands so inseparably connected as one and the same thing that we should find it difficult to get away from the fact that women did preach, or, in other words, prophesy, in the early ages of Christianity, and have continued to do so down to the present time to just the degree that the spirit of the Christian dispensation has been recognized. And it is also a significant fact that to the degree that denominations which have once favored the practice lose the freshness of their zeal, and, as a consequence, their primitive simplicity, and, as ancient Israel, yield to a desire to be like surrounding communities, in a corresponding ratio are the labors of females discountenanced.

Frances E. Willard, *Woman in the Pulpit*
(Boston: D. Lothrop Co., 1888), pp. 106–7

A Presbyterian woman gave this exegesis.

Men have interpreted and preached, and women have silently acquiesced, and have taken the place assigned to them from the pulpit, where the situation has not been rightly apprehended. From the third chapter of Genesis we understand that creation ceased when woman was made, leaving her in the ascending scale nearer to God in her gifts than the rest, and so fitted to be the moral guide of the race. That she has been so potent always, under all circumstances, for good or evil, should convince the doubting. The story of the fall is plain, though the logic of the translation is bad. However, the curse fell because of disobedience, and the curse fell on woman double, as she was the more responsible. Half her curse was that man should rule over her, showing by the new decree that there was a change in the relationship originally established. Any thoughtful mind can see the bitterness of her situation. The laws then laid down for her were for her punishment, proving nothing for her abilities or her relations, except as a culprit. The rules and Bible teaching through the old dispensation and the new, from that time, concern woman in her new position as culprit and prisoner, till the time be fulfilled, and do not, let me say again, define her original position, or sum up her abilities, any more than man's curse has to do with him in this way, or that of the Jews concerns them, but bears the same relation that the punishment of any State culprit does to the one concerned.

The inability on the part of teachers to rightly understand the situation has almost driven the question outside for settlement, and many intelligent mothers turn from the pulpit teachings on the subject, and look for relief to the educators and philanthropists.

Should not the teaching from the pulpit be this new statement showing what man's attitude towards his prisoner has been? Then may follow St. Paul's declaration of the continuance of the relation, showing what man's attitude towards his prisoner should be – the head, as Christ is head of the church. And how is that? He gave his life for it that he might finally present it without spot, or wrinkle, or any such thing, holy and without blemish. Under the old dispensation woman had nothing. Under the new, the crumbs that have fallen from man's table.

With these truths granted, that woman's position since sin entered the world by her is her punishment, and not her place, I think men will come to see where they have been hard taskmasters, and Christian men be shamed that Christianity has done so little for woman; that, instead of occupying her towards the position Christ occupied towards his church, giving her the best of his labor, and laying down his life for her good and advancement in every way, they have been more like Egyptian taskmasters, who required the full measure of bricks without furnishing the straw.

We come now to the consideration of woman's physical disabilities, the fact that she can be a mother being regarded as the crowning disability. Medical authority and statisticians declare that women have greater tenacity of life than men.

History shows that among the savage and heathen nations

(physically more normal than the civilized) maternity has not prevented women from bearing always the heaviest physical burdens. Christian lands have their own showing of mines and factories, and while I do not think that many nursing mothers would apply for admission to the pulpit, this position has not prevented them from letting their voices be heard from the other end of the church, oftentimes to greater comfort and edification than the voice of man is heard from the pulpit.

And notwithstanding the curse pronounced upon woman in the bearing of her children, mothers are able to stand and sing in choir, oratorio and opera, for a longer time than one could possibly listen to a sermon; so that neither lack of voice nor of physical strength can be offered against her appearing in the pulpit.

Frances E. Willard, Woman in the Pulpit
(Boston: D. Lothrop Co., 1888), pp. 107–9

These passages examine the basis of the preaching ministry of women in the Scriptures, the tradition and their own social context. The theology may be quaint, but the irony, particularly of the final, unnamed contributor, has weathered the test of time.
Frances Willard calls further witnesses.

Shall women preach? Certainly, if God calls them to preach. He cannot make a mistake. He is not the author of confusion. But will it not subvert the existing social order? If the existing social order is not in harmony with the divine plan, it will have to be subverted. Will it not make havoc with domestic relations and duties? It did not seem to do so in the case of Susannah Wesley, whom the learned Adam Clarke pronounced 'an able divine', and yet who held her nineteen children to a regimen as firm as that of West Point, though so gentle and tender that the same wise man writes of them: 'They had the reputation of being the most loving family in the country of Lincoln.' Catherine Booth has solved the same problem. Hardly Spurgeon himself is a better preacher or has a wider influence than she; yet her nine children are so loyal to her and her work they seem to think there is only one thing in the world worth doing, that is, to get everybody to Christ as soon as possible.

Quaker women have never found the question a difficult one. They have always been free to obey 'the inner voice;' and there are no lovelier women on the planet than those same gentle Friends, with their free step and well poised heads.

Through false Biblical interpretation the prejudices of the majority of the Lord's servants will bristle in woman's path like an *abatis*; and she will learn that she cannot argue down a prejudice. She may as well take the advice of good, wise old Sojourner Truth: 'What's de use o' makin' such a fuss about yer rights? Why dun ye jes' go 'long an' take 'em?'

No woman has ever, since the world began, been placed in a more public position than Queen Victoria; and yet, after fifty years of the fierce light that beats upon thrones, we read these words of her from a political opponent, the editor of the *Pall Mall Gazette*: –

This woman movement, so incalculable in its influence upon the future of our race, has undoubtedly been helped by a woman of high character and great common-sense. Her Majesty, from her earliest days, has accustomed the nation to the spectacle of a woman whose discharge of the highest political functions never impaired her womanliness, and who has been able to show, day by day, for fifty years, that the affairs of state, even when most engrossing, never interfered with the ideal of the wife and the mother, or destroyed the homeliness of the home.

We are not given to eulogize monarchs, and we fear the excessive laudation of the queen may provoke a reaction when the jubilee is over, but it is only common justice to admit that among the great silent influences which have worked for the emancipation of woman, few have been more potent than the spectacle, constantly before the eyes of all her people, of a woman crowned, yet womanly, the first politician in her land, and yet an ideal wife and mother, who, although the head of the greatest empire in the world, ever showed that her heart was centred in her home.

Frances E. Willard, *Woman in the Pulpit*
(Boston: D. Lothrop Co., 1888), pp. 109–11

Now some of these arguments will be familiar to those who have heard them advanced by those who oppose the ordination of women. What is less familiar is the testimony of the facts. Women have been preaching with an authentic and authoritative voice in a variety of contexts for well over a century. They have had to be defensive about this ministry, but equally they have exulted in it and done it extraordinarily well.

Frances Willard's collection of testimonies can be checked against other sources, all of which tell out the same story. Among these is an appreciation of the ministry of Susannah Wesley.

During the different periods of her husband's absence from home, there being no afternoon service at Epworth, Mrs. Wesley prayed with her own family on Sunday evenings, read a sermon, and engaged afterwards in religious conversation. Some of the parishioners who came in accidentally were not excluded; and she did not think it proper that their presence should interrupt the duty of the hour. Induced by the report which these persons made, others requested permission to attend; and in this manner from thirty to forty persons usually assembled. After this had continued some time, she happened to find an account of the Danish missionaries in her husband's study, and was much impressed by the perusal. The book strengthened her desire of doing good; she chose the best and most awakening of sermons, and spoke with more freedom, more warmth, more affection to the neighbours who attended at her evening prayers: their numbers increased in consequence, for she did not think it right to deny any who asked admittance. More persons came at length than the apartment could hold, and the thing was represented to her husband in such a manner, that he wrote to her, objecting to her conduct, because, he said, 'it looked particular' because of her sex, and because he was at that time in a public station, of a character which rendered it the more necessary that she should do nothing to attract censure, and he recommended that some other person should read for her. She began her reply by heartily thanking him for dealing so plainly and faithfully with her in a matter of no common concern. As to its 'looking particular,' she said, 'I grant it does, and so does almost everything that is serious, or that may any way advance the glory of God, or the salvation of souls, if it be performed out of a pulpit, or in the way of common conversation; because, in our corrupt age, the utmost care and diligence has been used to banish all discourse of God or spiritual concerns out of society, as if religion were never to appear out of the closet, and we were to be ashamed of nothing so much as of confessing ourselves to be Christians.' To the objection on account of her sex, she answered, that as she was a woman, so she was also mistress of a large family; and though the superior charge lay upon him as their head and minister, yet, in his absence, she could not but look upon every soul which he had left under her care, as a talent committed to her under a trust by the great Lord of all the families of heaven and earth. 'If,' she added, 'I am unfaithful to Him or to you, in neglecting to improve these talents, how shall I answer to Him when He shall command me to render an account of my stewardship?'

Mrs Ellis, *The Mothers of Great Men* (Edinburgh: W. P. Nimmo, Hay & Mitchell, 1902), pp. 324–5

A gloss on this text is provided by a comment from John Wesley, writing in 1791.

But conscience will not permit you to be silent when God commands you to speak. Yet I would have you give as little offence as possible; and, therefore, I would advise you not to speak at any place where a preacher is speaking at the same time, lest you should draw away his hearers.

John Wesley in Frances E. Willard, *Woman in the Pulpit* (Boston: D. Lothrop Co., 1888), p. 111

One hundred years later another of the contrary voices which women had to listen to was provided by John Angell James.

In short woman is everywhere to be found wrought into the detail of God's Scriptures, a beacon to warn us, or a lamp to guide us. And all the notices being written by the inspiration of the Holy

Spirit are to be considered as his testimony to the excellence and importance of your sex, and the influence it is intended and destined to exert upon the welfare of mankind. Had the Bible been against you, but had it passed you over in silence, or only referred to you incidentally, or looked at you; with sidelong glances, you would have sunk in general estimation; and man's neglect of you would have been defended or excused by that of God himself. But now no one can plead the example of the Bible for any attempt to neglect, despise, or oppress you. While it protects women from the insults, the injuries, and the oppression of the other sex, it saves her with no less care and benefit from the sad effects which would arise from the assumption of prerogatives which do not belong to her, and from those excesses of ambition to which her own vanity might otherwise prompt her. It guards her dignity from being trampled down by others, and equally prevents her from lowering it herself, by pretensions which would only make her ridiculous. It describes with accuracy the circle within which it is the will of Providence she should move; presents to her the mission which she is sent into the world to fulfil; furnishes her the rules by which she is to act; proposes to her the rewards which she may legitimately seek and surely expect, if she be faithful to herself; and offers her the assistance necessary for the fulfilment of her high and holy vocation.

> John Angell James, *Female Piety or the Young Woman's*
> *Friend and Guide through Life to Immortality*
> (London: Hamilton Adams & Co., 1877), pp. 53–4

This emotive language holds a snare. For the 'high and holy' vocation is too easily characterized as a call to silence. No campaigner was more outspoken in exposing this dynamic than Mrs General Booth.

There seems to be a great deal of unnecessary fear of women occupying any position which involves publicity, lest she should be rendered unfeminine by the indulgence of ambition or vanity, but why should woman any more than man be charged with ambition when impelled to use her talents for the good of her race? Moreover, as a labourer in the GOSPEL her position is much higher than in any other public capacity; she is at once shielded from all coarse and unrefined influences and associations; her very vocation tending to exalt and refine all the tenderest and most womanly instincts of her nature. As a matter of fact it is well known to those who have had the opportunities of observing the private character and deportment of women engaged in preaching the gospel, that they have been amongst the most amiable, self-sacrificing, and unobtrusive of their sex.

Catherine Booth, *Papers of Practical Religion*
(London: Salvation Army Book Stores, n.d.), pp. 96–7

Her biographer takes up the story.

In Hastings Mrs Booth met at the outset with considerable opposition. A band of Christian workers, who had been labouring there for some years past, were debating among themselves, in view of her anticipated visit, the propriety of a woman preaching, when one of their number, who had heard Mrs Booth, indignantly exclaimed that if such were their views they ought immediately to ask God to convert her into a man, rather than lose the benefits of her ministry.

F. de L. Booth-Tucker, *The Life of Catherine Booth: The Mother of the Salvation Army*, vol. 2 (London: The Salvation Army, 1891), p. 21

The Chatham News *in October 1873 was more enthusiastic.*

Mrs Booth possesses remarkable powers as a preacher. With a pleasing voice, distinct in all its tones, now colloquial, now persuasive, she can rise to the height of a great argument with an impassioned force and fervour that thrills her hearers. Quiet in her demeanour, her looks, her words, her actions are peculiarly emphatic. She can indeed 'suit the action to the word, the word to the action'. And yet there is no ranting – nothing to offend the most fastidious taste – but much to enchain attention. 'The matter is full, the manner excellent.'

The lady is engaged in a good work and we wish her God speed. We may safely prophesy that if she continues her addresses in Chatham the spacious lecture-hall will not contain those who wish to hear her.

F. de L. Booth-Tucker, *The Life of Catherine Booth: The Mother of the Salvation Army*, vol. 2 (London: The Salvation Army, 1891), p. 63

It is strange that a journalist should use the word 'quiet' about the demeanour of Mrs Booth. Here was a woman who could fill vast public buildings the world over, long before the advent of public address systems. Here was a woman who spoke on themes as varied as 'The Christs of the Nineteenth Century Compared with the Christ of God', 'A Mock Salvation and Real Deliverance from Sin', 'The Sham Judgement in Contrast with the Great White Throne', and whose Addresses to Business Gentlemen *were published by the Army.*

But the myths about silence were persuasive and reinforced by men who wrote at length about the proper duties and responses of men and women.

Meekness is a twin-sister of Peace. It is a temper of mind not easily provoked to resentment; or, as the word signifies, *easiness of mind*. The term for a meek man, used by the Romans, signified *used to hand*, in allusion to the taming of wild animals, which the cultivation of this grace truly resembles. It is the bringing of our wild and turbulent passions under control. It is an eminent work of the Spirit; and we may judge of our spiritual attainments by the degree of it which we possess. The Scriptures abound with exhortations to the cultivation of it. It is pre-eminently lovely in the female character. Hence Peter exhorts women to put on the ornament of a meek and quiet spirit, which is in the sight of God of great price.

H. Newcomb, *The Young Lady's Guide to the Harmonious Development of Christian Character* (London: T. Nelson & Sons, 1854), p. 32

His solution is an ingenious one.

As females are forbidden, by the dictates of nature and the word of God, to bear a part in the exercises of promiscuous and public meetings, it is highly proper, and very profitable, for them to hold meetings for prayer by themselves alone. We have reason to believe they did so in primitive times; for we read of a place by the river side, where prayer was wont to be made, and of the women who resorted thither. Such meetings exercise the gifts and graces of those who attend them, and serve to keep alive the flame of piety, as two or more brands placed together will preserve the fire, when, if left alone, they would all go out. Such meetings have been greatly blessed of God; and sometimes the flame of piety is kept alive in the female prayer-meeting, after it has apparently gone out on every other altar.

H. Newcomb, *The Young Lady's Guide to the Harmonious Development of Christian Character* (London: T. Nelson & Sons, 1854), p. 142

Christabel Pankhurst, the suffragette, would bring a note ·of realism to this debate.

Women are not of one mind on world problems, and there is no distinctive women's point of view concerning them. And if there were, it would still be true of women, as of men, that they have not the wisdom to devise the right policy. The power required is lacking too. Could women, as they cannot, tell the world what it is best to do in all these Age-old and now increasing and multiplying difficulties, there would still be the men to reckon with, and these might still prefer another and in their eyes better mode of action. Deadlock!

Christabel Pankhurst, *Pressing Problems of the Closing Age*
(London: Morgan & Scott Ltd, 1924), p. 42

This chapter has examined the rise of the woman preacher and some of the scriptural, theological and social issues that formed her context; the next must ask if – in spite of Christabel Pankhurst's claim – there is a distinctive 'women's point of view' to be discerned in what she had to say.

CHAPTER 4

～～

THE MEDIUM OF THE
DIVINE VOICE

'I will open my mouth in a parable; I will utter dark sayings
from of old' (Psalm 78.2)

Both in public and private Ann could read freely, not to say
fluently, from the Word of God, and the way the truth would flow
forth from her lips when speaking at her Father's bidding, was
'marvellous in our eyes'. While she found it utterly impossible to
memorize Scripture, yet she made it so constantly her meat and
drink that the Holy Spirit would bring to her remembrance just
the passage suited to the occasion. A great many can testify to the
aptness and point of the Scriptures that Ann would give on
different occasions. It was quite a common thing to request Ann
to ask her Father for a verse for them, and in a wonderful way,
after lifting up her eyes and her heart heavenward, Ann would
give forth some passage which was evidently most suited to the
special need; in fact without knowing the circumstances, she
became repeatedly the medium of the Divine voice either to
guide, comfort or correct those who thus sought her ministry.

Helen E. Bingham, *An Irish Saint*
(London: Morgan & Scott Ltd, n.d.), pp. 79–80

*The earliest of the women preachers were often known as
prophetesses. This is a title they bore with pride, in the certainty
that they were given to the Church in order to 'guide, comfort or
correct' those who sought out their ministry. In our own times,*

Miriam

however, it requires some examination. Does the wisdom which women preachers bring to the public discourse of the churches place them as teachers, or does it cast them in the role of purveyors of 'dark secrets'? In what does the darkness of these secrets lie? Why did their ministry first provoke a fearful reaction in people? Why did it require the justification and advocacy we have examined in Chapter 3?

Women commentators such as Helen Bingham, in her account of the prophetic ministry of Ann Preston, make no apology. The Methodist writer Dora Greenwell is also prepared to discern the presence of the Spirit in confronting 'indifference and formalism'.

When the universal Christian heart grows strong enough to burst through its band of indifference and formalism, a body will be prepared for it, we know not yet under what conditions of strength and freedom. Prophecy seems to point to a great increase of spiritual energy in the Church before the time of our Lord's second coming, the time of the 'latter rain', which will be given abundantly; nor do we know what channels may be now preparing for the risen waters, waters to swim in, a river not to be passed over, which shall go down into the desert and into the sea, and which being brought forth into the sea, the waters 'shall be healed'.

Dora Greenwell, *Two Friends*
(London: The Epworth Press, 1952), p. 120

In common with many of the other women preachers, she writes eloquently about the gift of the Spirit to the churches and identifies the prophetic tradition as a source of spiritual energy. One way in which this gift is revealed is through the call to preach. These writers are confident that this ministry would bring healing to the Church. They offer words 'in a parable', in the words of Psalm 78. What they did not anticipate was that they would be heard and perceived as offering 'dark secrets'. For what they sometimes fail to see is that these parables can be misinterpreted as a radical call to subversion through the gift of freedom.

The Moravian, Sister Eva of Friedenshort, takes up the same theme.

The whole eighth chapter of Romans is really a triumph song of the freedom purchased for us in Christ and appropriated through the Holy Spirit. We do not any longer need to be slaves of sin, but may rejoice in the liberty that Christ gives. Under the law of sin we are poor, enslaved, bound, hemmed in, oppressed, and shackled people. Under Grace, in the sphere of the might of the Holy Spirit, the fetters fall through His emancipating power. We have the possibility of leading a holy life, and may rejoice and be comforted in this deliverance from the tyranny of sin. Zinzendorf says: 'It is our privilege that we are not obliged to sin.' Not, that we *cannot* sin! But we *need* not, we are not obliged to. We *can* *overcome* in Him, the great Overcomer, Who will sanctify us if we walk in the liberty that has been given us, and neither lose nor sell it for the sake of anything that the Enemy offers.

Sister Eva of Friedenshort, The Working of the Holy Spirit in Daily Life
(London: Hodder & Stoughton, 1933), pp. 90–1

The theological insight into the role of the Spirit as a gift of freedom is further developed here. 'We can overcome in Him, the great Overcomer.' When the theological reflection of women is applied through the medium of words, it has a twofold edge to it. First, it aspires to be real and rooted – which means that it has the potential to become political. That is why Sister Eva sees the Holy Spirit alive and active in the 'working of daily life'. Second, it names God – rather than man – as the ultimate source of freedom. Another sister, simply called Emily, dedicated her collection of writings to 'the fortunate Eves who have not confided too far in Adams'.

This chapter will examine these two threads in the prophetic, Spirit-filled ministry of the women preachers. It must, however, face the obvious question about their ministry. Were their secrets so very dark, and what, if any, is their wisdom for our own times? It has to be said that the tag 'dark' is one which women preachers will always find it hard to shift. To the outsider they will look totally orthodox; it is within the fold that their troubles start. The outsider in this instance is Leonora Eyles, a careers consultant.

The Free Churches have for some considerable time admitted women actually to the ministry; this is a very special profession, demanding great gifts and entailing an arduous training. Like the Church of England, the Free Churches admit women as deaconesses, and their work is both preaching and social work in the district they serve. These are not jobs which anyone can take on; a profound religious belief and faith in the inspiration and need for the work are needed. But here, too, there is a demand for lay workers in the Sunday schools, social clubs, and in missionary efforts for the foreign field; here too the women do valiant work in caring for the babies during gatherings of young mothers, in catering for parties and other social functions and in performing those 'good-neighbourly' acts which I have mentioned in connection with the Church of England. Anyone who comes into any Christian Church – if it is alive at all – cannot but be struck by the friendliness of these women; they welcome 'outsiders' and make them feel at home and soon find them something to do: such a good way of getting rid of embarrassment and of combating loneliness.

Leonora Eyles, *Unmarried but Happy*
(London: Victor Gollancz Ltd, 1947), p. 136

Leonora's is the sound voice of reason. She makes the obvious connections between what is happening in the Churches and what is happening elsewhere.

The question of masculine jealousy cuts into women's occupations all along the line; in many hospitals women students are literally physically shoved out of the way by male students during clinical rounds and in the operating theatre; while it is well known that a woman surgeon has still great difficulty in fighting her way to hospital appointments, and must, in order to compete for a post with men, possess much higher qualifications than they, while in general practice there is still some prejudice to fight. The Church of England still bars women from even voluntary service at her altars, although several eminent Churchmen are beginning to ask why, and although the Nonconformist Church had already 147 women ministers in 1924. In a book on sex written by a well-known Churchman in 1930, it was stated that a general sex complex would always keep women from Holy Orders, because women, being more intimately connected with the processes of sex than men, were therefore less pure and clean, and therefore unfit to touch holy things. In journalism, women, no matter how highly qualified, are generally relegated to 'women's page stuff' and the man editor of a women's page recently told me that he could not find women with enough brains and education to supply him with the copy he wanted. We have no woman 'star' reporter of the calibre of, say, H. V. Morton of the *Daily Express*, although in the freer fields of fiction and travel books women have proved their undoubted ability as descriptive writers; we have no woman editor of a daily paper, although women have shown what they can do in smaller and privately owned periodicals; in educational circles women still work at a much lower scale of pay than men. Only in commerce and advertising do we hear of women being appointed to posts at anything like the same salaries as men, and being given a chance of work of real scope and responsibility.

Leonora Eyles, *Careers for Women*
(London: Elkin Mathews & Marrot, 1930), pp. 19–20

Leonora Eyles here identifies the opposition to the ministry of women. Her clarity on the question of male jealousy is attractive. Would that it were that simple. For motivation is hard to establish when it dresses up as theological truth. If anything, her observations about being 'pure and clean' are even more telling. Are Spirit-filled women preachers pure vessels of election, or are they closer to the sibyls of old? Harmonious Christian character is too easily equated with a questionable kind of hygiene.

It is also essential to cultivate personal cleanliness. There is an *odour* in this insensible perspiration, which become offensive when the impurities collecting upon the surface of the skin are not frequently removed. The entire surface of the body should be washed every day; and, if this is done on rising in the morning, with cold water, and followed by brisk rubbing with a coarse towel, it will furnish an effectual safeguard against taking cold. This, however, should be omitted when there is any danger to be apprehended from the sudden application of cold, or serious consequences may follow. Warm water, with soap, should occasionally be used at night, in order to remove all impurities from the skin.

H. Newcomb, *The Young Lady's Guide to the Harmonious Development of Christian Character* (London: T. Nelson & Sons, 1854), p. 170

There is a subtle contrast between this warning about unclean-ness and the evangelical enthusiasm of Eugenia Price's advice on careful grooming to the Lord.

My eyes go involuntarily to two points of a woman's anatomy when I meet her. Her hands and her teeth. Glamorous, long, regularly formed nails and white even rows of teeth are found only rarely except in the ads for toothpaste and nail polish. But teeth can be clean and nails can be clean and both can, and must be, regularly cared for if we are to be good for the reputation of Jesus Christ in our daily contacts.

Quite sometime ago I learned that after thirty minutes of talking, the human throat dries out to such an extent that the breath is bad as a consequence. As regular a part of the mysterious contents of my purse as a comb, is a bottle of breath sweetener or a roll of mints: No one is safe from offending in this way. The slightest tip one way or another in our body chemistry, from fatigue, overeating, or overtalking can cause halitosis. And quite often lack of proper dental care causes it. The use of dental floss and a rubber massage tip on your toothbrush will help wonder-fully.

I am very much aware that you already know these things. I am not writing this book for bush women. I am writing it for you. And I am writing as I am in this chapter more as a reminder that we owe careful grooming to the Lord as part of obedience. Polish your shoes, clean your galoshes, shampoo your hair, care for your skin and nails and teeth, and bathe frequently to the glory of God!

All of these things, too, can be meaningful sacraments if we really love Christ.

Eugenia Price, *Woman to Woman*
(Grand Rapids: Zondervan, 1959), p. 79

The 'bush woman' tag is similar to the 'dark secret's' tag. Arthur Newsholme makes the connection.

In classical mythology, Aesculapius was worshipped as the god of Medicine, while his daughter Hygeia had homage done to her as the sweet and smiling goddess of Health. The temples of these two deities were always placed in close contiguity; and statues representing Hygeia were often placed in the temple of Aesculapius. In these statues she is represented as a beautiful maiden holding in her hand a bowl, from which a serpent is drinking – the serpent typifying the art of medicine, then merely an art, now establishing its right more and more to the dignity of a science.

Arthur Newsholme, *Hygiene: A Manual of Personal and Public Health*
(London: George Gill & Sons, 1892), p. 7

Now 'classical antiquity' is a polite term for the 'pagan world'. Part of the opposition to women's role as preachers comes from a form of Christianity which can only understand itself in terms of its opposition to the pagan world. The woman who has access to dark secrets is a servant of the pagan temple, not a true daughter of God. Therefore she must be opposed because she represents the dark forces of nature, rather than the bright forces of reason and culture. When women preachers revealed an extraordinary familiarity with the Bible, when they spoke artlessly about the gift of the Spirit and the call to freedom, they could still be heard with suspicion and fear.

For that reason they had a high investment in preaching an orthodox gospel. Indeed the only way to expose the myth about their access to 'dark secrets' was for God to call forward some extraordinarily orthodox and mainstream women preachers. The testimony of the greatest of these makes precisely this point. In

57

1936 Maude Royden went to Canada. The Toronto Daily Star *of 30 July 1936 takes up the story.*

Miss Agnes Maude Royden, D.D., graduate of Oxford (Doctor of Divinity from the University of Glasgow), late associate preacher of London's greatest preaching fane, the City Temple, is the greatest woman preacher in the English tongue in the annals of the English-speaking world. And as lecturer and author her name stands among women's foremost few.

Deer Park United church, Toronto, is, for the next month or so, to echo to her voice – and it was within the vestry of that tabernacle today, that I (who have myself sat at her distinguished feet in old London) was privileged to speak with our welcome guest.

'How did you come to choose preaching as a calling?' I pursued. 'I never did – it chose me. I began my public speaking career in the interests of the Woman's Suffrage movement. How it flowered into the religious, I myself hardly know.'

'Are you the only Doctor of Divinity in captivity?', I queried.

'Yes,' she smiled, 'I believe that is so – Glasgow University is responsible for that.'

The Guildhouse Monthly,
Vol. 10, No. 107, September 1936, p. 207

So much for the commentators, but what did Maude Royden have to say about her own ministry?

So – to be personal for a moment – when I first began to preach, I felt very strongly that people ought not to treat sex as though it were of eternal significance; that the things of the spirit should be proclaimed by men and women alike; that if God gave a message to any human being, she should not be forbidden to deliver it, because she was a woman. That I still deeply and passionately feel.

But I have also learned that there is, notwithstanding, a certain point of view which will enable women to give to the world not only in practical service but in theology – in the world's idea of

God Himself – some fresh understanding, some new light. After all, it does matter in what kind of body your spirit is enshrined. The point of view (as I have said already) of India, of China, of Africa and of America has a certain difference, and we all feel – those of us who think of it at all – that our understanding of Christ and of God is not complete until every race has brought its peculiar spiritual genius, and its special spiritual experience, to the understanding of our great and universal religion.

In the same way, I have become convinced that from their actual experience, from the fact that to be a woman gives one a rather different angle of vision to certain things in life, something can be given even to our conception of God Himself, some new understanding of the great teaching of Christ, when women begin to take their full share in thinking out their faith. Women have always been among the great saints, the great servants of Humanity, the practical Christians; but, on the whole, the theology of the world is the work of men. There have been a few great women theologians, a Catherine of Siena, a Teresa of Spain, but these women have always been the exceptional women, the women whose experience, so far as that is possible, has rather been like the experience of a man than the experience of the normal woman. That is to say, they have not been wives and mothers, and though motherhood has been in them expressed spiritually their contribution to theology has been rather more like that of a great man, in some respects, than representative of the experience of the normal, average – I use the word in its best sense – woman's life. It is this particular contribution to theology, not that of the exceptional woman, but that of the woman whose life is pre-eminently that of her sex, that I believe is going to add such wealth of understanding to the theology of this generation.

A. Maude Royden, *Women at the World's Crossroads*
(New York: The Woman's Press, 1922), pp. 79–80

Maude Royden is aware that women have something new to contribute to the making of theology. But she sees this happening in the future, at some time when the experience of women will inspire the theology of a new generation. Many of her sermons are slight in

content, although they were faithfully published in the Guildhouse
Monthly. *What cannot be captured in the pages of a book is the
sound of her voice, however; and those who remember hearing her
speak, or who have heard her voice from archived broadcasts held
by the BBC, all claim that her voice was enchanting because it
was energetic and clear. There was a new sound around in the
making of theology, and the Nonconformists (because they were
among the first to accept the preaching ministry of women) would
be the first to hear it.*

*Joan Mary Fry, of the Religious Society of Friends, had already
hinted at this in her Swarthmore Lecture of 1910.*

Quakerism is nothing unless it be a communion of life, a practical
showing that the spiritual and material spheres are not divided,
but are as the concave and convex sides of one whole, and that the
one is found in and through the other. It emphasises the fact that
the Church is a body of common men and women, that worship is
part of living, and that the whole of life is sacramental and
incarnational. Its function is to show that this mystical position is
strong in that the essence of Christian beauty is distilled out of
accepted difficulties, harmonised discords, and visions of good
hidden in things evil. The spiritual is extracted from the material;
and nothing is cast to the waste void. Above all, it must be made
clear that the power to attain this is the inheritance of every one,
that none may be debarred from it, but that it is free and patent to
all. This should be done if the Society is to make good its claim to
build a spiritual home without specialist aid, out of the simple
materials of ordinary human nature.

Joan Mary Fry, *The Communion of Life*
(London: Headley Brothers, 1910), pp. 10–11

*Theology may be built out of experience. With the admission of
women to the preaching ministry of the Church, the base of this
experience was broadened. But so too was the base of reaction to
it. For the voice of women which was now heard in the pulpit
would take up an agenda for social, as well as theological, change.
It is not by chance that Maude Royden associated her call to*

preaching with the work of the suffragette movement. For the connectedness of the 'simple materials of ordinary human nature' would now be explored in the public as well as the private domain.

Does this mean that women should only teach about the home or about social issues? Should they only preach about other women? The evidence runs counter to this. The oldest of the Christian mysteries were tackled fearlessly by the likes of a Dorothy L. Sayers.

All of us, perhaps, are too ready, when our behaviour turns out to have appalling consequences, to rush out and hang ourselves. Sometimes we do worse, and show an inclination to go and hang other people. Judas, at least, seems to have blamed nobody but himself, and St. Peter who had a minor betrayal of his own to weep for, made his act of contrition and waited to see what came next. What came next for St. Peter and the other disciples was the sudden assurance of what God was, and with it the answer to all the riddles.

If Christ could take evil and suffering and do that sort of thing with them, then of course it was all worth while and the triumph of Easter linked up with that strange triumphant prayer in the Upper Room, which the events of Good Friday had seemed to make so puzzling. As for their own parts in the drama, nothing could now alter that they had been stupid, cowardly, faithless, and in many ways singularly unhelpful; but they did not allow any morbid and egotistical remorse to inhibit their joyful activities in the future.

Now, indeed, they could go out and 'do something' about the problem of sin and suffering. They had seen the strong hands of God twist the crown of thorns into a crown of glory, and in hands as strong as that they knew themselves safe. They had misunderstood practically everything Christ had ever said to them, but no matter: the thing made sense at last, and the meaning was far beyond anything they had dreamed. They had expected a walkover, and they beheld a victory; they had expected an early Messiah, and they beheld the Soul of Eternity.

It had been said to them of old time, 'No man shall look upon My face and live'; but for them a means had been found. They had seen the face of the living God turned upon them; and it was the face of a suffering and rejoicing Man.

Dorothy L. Sayers, *Creed or Chaos?*
(London: Methuen & Co. Ltd, 1947), pp. 12–13

This universal theological reflection on the work of the Redeemer is matched by reflection on the work of the Comforter. These texts are important because they demonstrate that women preachers rapidly became interested in the ways in which God is named and identified.

And here, I think, we have especial need of the work of the Comforter. When we have received the witness of the Spirit bearing witness with our Spirit that we are the children of God, and if children, then heirs, our experience works hope, and gives us, as it were, ground to stand upon in heaven. Then they who have received the Earnest know enough of the Inheritance, and of Him in whom they have obtained it, to see clearly that spiritual and eternal life are identical. All renewed life, being one with that of the Renewer, is one life; the same life, whether its outward circumstances be more or less happy – whether, in short, it be spent in heaven above, or upon earth below. And to speak of our present and our future life in Christ as being in any way separate from each other, is to draw a distinction which our Lord Himself is most careful to avoid.

Dora Greenwell, *Covenant of Life and Peace*
(London: H. R. Allenson Ltd, n.d.), p. 97

The very nature of God is subject to scrutiny and review in these texts. God is the Comforter, the Earnest, the Renewer by turns. So who would be comforted and renewed by God? The abiding legacy of the women preachers – as of the hymn-writers – is not that there are still women preaching and writing hymns. It would go far beyond that. Because their word would also become flesh. God, newly named and known, would reach out and comfort and renew a new generation. In Maude Royden's words, 'What are we to do with our freedom? What special gifts have we with which to serve our country and the world?'

CHAPTER 5

~~

HOUSEHOLD LORE

'When I thought to understand this, it seemed to me a wearisome
task, until I went into the sanctuary of God' (Psalm 73.17)

*The writings in this chapter once again find women at an
interface. This time it is between the series of 'wearisome tasks'
which they encounter when cast in role and the sense of personal
glory to which they also aspire and will meet in the sanctuary of
God. This is a subtle interface. It is not simply about equating
domestic life with everything that is wearisome, and public life
with glory. It is about access to the sanctuary – to the holy –
wherever it may be encountered. In order to achieve this access,
the women preachers and other theologians had to become
campaigners. An important element in their campaign was the
attention they brought to examining the traditional roles of women
as cooks, cleaners and carers. It is these which this chapter will
examine. Chapter 6 will take up the same threads and investigate
how they informed the political and social campaigning of women.*

*We have seen Catherine Booth at the rostrum. Now we meet her
in her own home.*

Very inexperienced in household lore was Mrs Bramwell Booth at
the outset of her married life, but the help and advice of Mrs
General Booth was of inestimable service to her. As the elder Mrs
Booth had united with such notable success the duties of public
evangelist to those of a devoted wife and mother, so she guided
her first daughter-in-law to follow in the same steps. 'It was she
who showed me,' said Mrs Booth recently to a friend, 'that my
home was part of my life-work, and that in tackling home

difficulties and doing everything there as well as it could possibly be done, I was glorifying God as much as if I were leading a meeting. This gave me great peace and rest in the early years when my life was all behind the scenes, and it fitted me also for my future.'

A lady who has been intimately acquainted with Mrs Bramwell Booth for many years testifies that 'she unites remarkable gifts of practical common-sense and judgement with great force of character, and yet with a singularly gentle and quiet manner, and may we not add that her example of simplicity and devotion, and inflexible adherence to principle, no less than her whole-hearted Salvationism, has won for her a wide influence both within the Salvation Army and outside its borders?'

Clara Lucas Balfour, *Women Worth Emulating*
(London: Sunday School Union, 1907), pp. 152–3

Now the Booth women were strong candidates for the kind of challenge Maude Royden would lay down.

Women to whom your Saviour made appeal as no other great Founder of religion has done, and who have responded to it as to no other, witnessing as evangelists, dying as martyrs for your faith, now is the hour for you to witness once again. In every aspect of it your age-old experience of life has fitted you for the task. As life-bearers, as the guardians of children, the makers of homes, as newcomers in world affairs, as long-sufferers of violence you had no power to resist, as the world's drudges, as the half-worshipped mothers of men, as souls for whom Christ died, as saints who died for him, give now to a sick and fainting world what you best can give – new hope, new life.

A. Maude Royden, *Women's Partnership in the New World*
(London: George Allen & Unwin Ltd, 1941), pp. 140–1

What is the difference between the note of hope and confidence which is struck by Maude Royden and the troubling and contrary voices which also whispered in women's ears?

65

SPECIMEN WEEKLY HOUSEKEEPING ACCOUNT

	Sun.		Mon.		Tues.		Wed.		Thur.		Fri.		Sat.		Total		
	s.	d.	s.	d.	s.	d.	s.	d.	s.	d.	s.	d.	s.	d.	£	s.	d.
Butcher							2	0			5	6				7	6
Baker				8		8	2	4				8	4	6		8	10
Milkman													4	8		4	8
Greengrocer					1	2			2	9			9	6		13	5
Grocer			3	6			2	0					15	0	1	0	6
Fishmonger					1	6			1	3	3	6				6	3
Laundry													6	0		6	0
Clothes											7	6				7	6
Fares and Lunches	15	0														15	0
Recreation (including Cigarettes and Drinks)	5	0	3	6					3	6	7	0				19	0
	20	0	7	8	3	4	9	10	4	0	24	2	39	8	5	8	8

Items allowed for but not yet paid or paid in advance—	£	s.	d.
Rent and Rates	2	10	0
Electricity and Gas		3	6
Hire-Purchase	1	10	0
Coal used		5	0
Insurances		2	6
	£9	19	8

The world never owned such opulence of womanly character, or such splendour of womanly manners or multitudinous instances of wifely, motherly, daughterly, sisterly devotion, as it owns today. I have not words to express my admiration for good womanhood. Woman is not only man's equal, but in affectional and religious nature – which is the best part of us – she is seventy-five per cent his superior. Yea, during the last twenty years, through the increased opportunity opened for female education, the women of the country are better educated than the majority of men; and if they continue to advance in mentality at the present ratio, before long the majority of men will have difficulty in finding in the opposite sex enough ignorance to make appropriate consorts. If I am under a delusion as to the abundance of good womanhood abroad, consequent upon my surroundings, since the hour I entered this life until now, I hope the delusion will last until I embark from this planet.

T. DeWitt Talmage, *Marriage and Home Life*
(Edinburgh: Oliphant, Anderson & Ferrier, 1886), pp. 8–9

The snare of passages such as these is that they use seductive language to praise women: 'woman is not only man's equal . . . she is seventy-five per cent his superior'. All of this is a long way away from the cool voice of reason which Kathleen Bliss would bring to bear on the question of women's dignity within relationships.

Women also had a high status in Anglo-Saxon Britain. Women, especially women of noble birth, were the first converts to the Christian faith and took up from the missionaries, from whom they learned, the task of evangelising their tribes. It was Queen Bertha who made to St. Augustine and his followers the grant of land on which to build the cathedral of Canterbury: and many are the stories of tribal queens and princesses suffering martyrdom for the new faith. Soon religious houses for women were established in Anglo-Saxon England, and even mixed houses (separate departments of a single religious community). At the close of the seventh century there were five such mixed houses in Kent alone, all governed by women. In the councils of the Church the position of honour given to Abbesses was next to that of Bishops. St. Hilda presided at the great Synod of Whitby in 664, and five abbesses put their names to the Acts of the Great Council of Beckenham in 694.

It is easy of course to exaggerate the place occupied by women in the Church in past ages. The plain fact is that with rare, and for the most part modern exceptions, all clergy are men and the highest offices of the Church – all Churches – are occupied by the clergy. In saying that there have been periods when women have held a high and honoured place in the Church, it is not meant that down the course of history now men and now women have had the major share in shaping the course of the Church's life. That is not true. The guiding hands have always been masculine. But what is true is that at some periods women who have felt the call of God to serve Him and their fellows, have found a means of fulfilling that vocation in the Church and at other times the Church has had no room for them, no belief in their 'call', no encouragement and guidance in the fulfilment of it. Women have never found their place in the Church by imposing their views: whether they find

fulfilment or frustration depends on the relationship of the sexes –
not only the relation of an individual man and an individual
woman in marriage but the total relationship, governed by what
men think of women, how they behave towards them and what
women think of themselves. The question of the place of women
in the Churches is not a 'women's question'. It might more truly
be called a 'men's question'. Fundamentally it is a question of
relationship.

Kathleen Bliss, *The Service and Status of Women in the Churches*
(London: SCM Press Ltd, 1952), pp. 15–16

*The authority with which Kathleen Bliss writes, as well as her
clarity, can be capped by the insight of another prolific woman
writer. Evelyn Underhill's concern is the 'splendour of God',
which*

. . . the Divine Wisdom irradiated once and irradiates still. It
means a new quality of life possible to us and awaiting us; not
somewhere else, but where we are now.

This quality of life is already manifest, wherever limiting forms
of human devotion, human suffering, human service are given in
simplicity to the total purpose of God. For Reality has been
shown to us incarnate among men, so that we may try to weave its
pattern into the texture of human life; redeeming that life from
ugliness, and making it a garment of God. It is not a conspicuous
pattern. The shimmer of holiness appears upon the surface
mostly in obscure acts of sacrifice and quiet selfless deeds. But
when we look behind, and trace this delicate beauty to its source,
what we see is a living Love; so individual and yet so general, that
on one hand the relation of each spirit to that Spirit is unique and
complete, and on the other the love poured out on one subtracts
nothing from the love given to all. We taste then, in our limited
way, something of that experience which transfigured the
Twelve, imparted to them the life-giving life, and sent them out
to spread it through the world.

And indeed, the Christian is required for this and for no other
purpose; to be one more worker for the Kingdom, one more

transmitter of the Divine Charity, the great spendthrift action of God.

Evelyn Underhill, *The School of Charity*
(London: Longmans, Green & Co., 1934), pp. 70–1

Bliss and Underhill talk about the importance of relationships and the quality of life. These can be nurtured both within the home and beyond. So much for the easy rhetoric of T. DeWitt Talmage.

What the world wants now is about fifty thousand old-fashioned mothers, women who shall realise that the highest, grandest, mightiest institution on earth is the home. It is not necessary that they should have the same old-time manners of the country farmhouse, or wear the same old-fashioned spectacles and apron that her glorified ancestry wore; but I mean the old spirit which began with the Hannahs and the Mother Lois and the Abigails of Scripture days, and was demonstrated on the homestead where some of us were reared, though the old house long ago was pulled down and its occupants scattered, never to meet until in the higher home that awaits the families of the righteous. While there are more good and faithful wives and mothers now than there ever were, society has got a wrong twist on this subject, and there are influences abroad that would make women believe that their chief sphere is outside instead of inside the home.

T. DeWitt Talmage, *Marriage and Home Life*
(Edinburgh: Oliphant, Anderson & Ferrier, 1886), p. 104

Even Mrs Sumner, who founded the Mothers' Union and whose theology of marriage veered to the conservative, would avoid such generalizations. Where Talmage always admonishes wives, her address is directed 'To Husbands'.

Christianity brings us personally to Christ, and dignifies every relationship in life. Christianity teaches us that marriage is a sacred bond, that is the basis of all true home life, and the nation should do everything to preserve the Home as the chief training place of the future men and women of England.

We appeal to every true Englishman and we ask him to bear in mind, that as the foundation of home-life is holy marriage, it should be treated seriously and reverently. 'For this cause shall a man leave his Father and Mother, and cleave to his wife, and they twain shall be one flesh.'

I fear many homes in this land are not founded on this divine principle of love and mutual service.

Mrs Sumner, *Home Life*
(London: Wells Gardner, Darton & Co., n.d.), p. 139

'Love and mutual service' are to be offered by both women and men. As social change, education and war brought women new experiences, so too they had the opportunity to reflect upon the applicability of such mutuality. Maude Royden tackled the underlying questions about difference and subordination.

The assumption that man was the norm inclined women to show that they could be as square as he. Any difference was assumed by men to be an inferiority, and by some women at least was slurred over and minimized as far as possible. But it remains a fact that women are different from men in certain respects, and, neither minimizing nor maximizing this difference, should simply take it into account, and demand conditions which suit them. If men and women are working together and conditions cannot be made ideal for both, there should be a compromise. At present the 'compromise' is apt to consist in the convenience of men being considered, and the inconvenience of women endured in silence due to an 'inferiority' in their natures.

A. Maude Royden, *The Making of Women*
(London: George Allen & Unwin Ltd, 1917), p. 129

The actual nature of the home as a working environment is best considered by an expert such as Elizabeth Atkinson.

An immense objective, indeed, reveals itself as the goalpoint of this branch of the work. The 'compleat housewife' is to be turned out competent to accomplish every piece of work that goes towards the management of a home. She must be able to cook and store food, make, mend, and launder clothes and house linen; she must know how to clean not only the whole of the house itself but also every conceivable household appurtenance within and without its bounds; she must be capable of choosing and purchasing food, fuel, cleaning materials, clothing, furniture, furnishings and house decorations, and should be an adept at keeping accounts; she must know something about sites and situations of houses, and must understand their drainage, sanitation, ventilation, and various lighting and heating systems; she should possess a knowledge of how to bring up infants and children and of how to tend the sick and administer first aid in the case of accidents; she must be able to execute simple household repairs and renovations and to use stains, varnishes, paints, and enamels. Her work must be characterized by efficiency, punctuality, strict hygiene, and orderliness; by an artistic touch and by gentleness of movement; she should be capable of acting aright in an emergency, and must be able to maintain the simultaneous smooth-running of the innumerable sections of household machinery, herself keeping, in accordance with old tradition, 'above all of good temper'. Moreover, now that she is an enfranchised woman, she must find enough time and leisure in which to acquaint herself with politics and municipal government, so that as an experienced home-maker she may have a deciding voice in these matters where they touch questions connected with the home.

Elizabeth Atkinson, *The Teaching of Domestic Science*
(London: Methuen & Co. Ltd., 1931), pp. 24–5

This list of accomplishments makes daunting reading. It provides a clue, though, to discovering which of their achievements women would bring out from the home and apply in the outer world. The pattern is threefold: cooking, cleaning and caring. The nurturing of relationships and quality of life identified by Kathleen Bliss and Evelyn Underhill are matched by a preoccupation with cleanli-

ness and with the care of the sick. Instead of being told by men that they should keep their homes clean, women would start to tell men to clean up their lives. Instead of being told that they should care for the sick, they began to ask questions about the causes of sickness. Domestic science would become a political science.

The importance of cleanliness has already been seen as an obstacle for women as they first approached the pulpit and altar. Now it crops up in the domestic context.

It is duty to pay some regard to personal appearance. A Christian lady, by making herself a *slattern* brings reproach upon the cause of Christ, instead of glorifying God. The apostle enjoins upon women to adorn themselves with *modest* apparel. Modesty signifies *purity of purpose and manners*. When this idea is applied to dress, it immediately suggests to the mind a neatness, taste, and simplicity, alike opposed both to extravagance and finery, and to negligence and vulgar coarseness. The exercise of a refined taste, in the adaption and adjustment of apparel, may also be justified by the analogy of nature. Look abroad over the landscape, and see with what exquisite taste God has clothed the flowers of the field. There is a symmetry of proportion, a skilfullness of arrangement, and a fitness and adaption of colours, which strike the eye with unmingled pleasure. And if God has shown a scrupulous regard to the pleasure of the eye, we may do the same. This opinion is also confirmed by the practical influence of the gospel.

H. Newcomb, *The Young Lady's Guide to the Harmonious Development of Christian Character* (London: T. Nelson & Sons, 1854), pp. 250–2

The scripts are persuasive. Cleanliness rapidly becomes equated with 'purity of purpose and manners'. There were other ways of interpreting the same information, as Elizabeth Atkinson would reveal.

As regards fabrics, modern invention has played into the hands of the housewife in giving her artificial silk that is not only washed and finished with ease, but which, by reason of its high gloss, is a fine dirt-resisting fabric; and recent improvements in the manufacture of shantung and tussore silks have produced many garments which entail the minimum of labour in laundering. Then, again, multi-coloured cretonnes, unstarched repps, and the like now cover chairs and settees instead of the chintzes of fifty years ago, which necessitated that back-breaking process known 'callendering'.

In view of the interaction between supply and demand it would thus appear that the legitimate desire of the housewife for a less arduous washing day is creating a market supply of goods which by reason of the nature of their fabric and their construction tend to reduce labour in the home. To the female community in general a blessing and a boon is thus effected, for many a family wash that has been tackled by a woman has been compatible with the strength of a robust man; and even to-day, despite the more simply constructed garments, the more easily laundered fabrics, and the labour-saving washing devices of recent invention, a twentieth-century washing day is by no means free from its aftermath of fatigue and jading on the part of the housewife.

Elizabeth Atkinson, *The Teaching of Domestic Science*
(London: Methuen & Co. Ltd., 1931), p. 22

The pursuit of cleanliness debilitated even the most robust of women because it was jading work. But the pursuit of cleanliness is an important key to understanding the motivation of the social purity campaigners of the late-nineteenth century, as Cecilia Ady became aware.

The early moral welfare workers were compelled by sympathy to promote all that could be done to rescue those who were suffering from the results of a double moral standard for men and women, but a few of them went further and challenged a public opinion which was based on it and which tolerated both in law and custom gross injustices towards the victims of this system.

To realise the magnitude of the work accomplished by Mrs. Josephine Butler and her colleagues, it must be remembered that she opposed a system supported by the medical opinion of the time, and by the majority of the clergy, lawyers, politicians and

73

officials in every European country. When she led a campaign against attempts to regulate prostitution by the Contagious Diseases Acts passed in 1864–9, the reverberations of her attack echoed throughout Europe.

Cecilia M. Ady, *The Role of Women in the Church*
(London: The Central Council for Women's Church Work, 1948), p. 60

So the insights of the wash tub were reclaimed by women. Purity and cleanliness would no longer be used against them; instead – as the next chapter will reveal – they would go to the barricades in defence of a new and more just morality. Even at a personal level, though, the language and gestures of water would be reclaimed by women.

Years ago, a rather 'churchy' young woman, I was shocked when a dear friend told me that she had for various personal reasons ceased to go to church, but that she made her devotions in the morning while she was taking her bath, 'And then I start the day clean and refreshed inside and outside,' she added. Like Brother Lawrence, she had discovered the 'practice of the presence of God' and carried that presence everywhere with her; she had a very curious effect on me, as on many in a very large organisation in which we both worked. Her office was a little glass room amongst many others, and my work, very harassing at times, carried me past her office frequently. Just looking at her bending over her desk made me feel calm and happy, even before I knew her well, and others told me the same thing about her.

Leonora Eyles, *Unmarried but Happy*
(London: Victor Gollancz Ltd, 1947), pp. 121–2

This interpretation is matched by theological reflection too.

Baptism is the being 'begotten unto a lively hope', it is the sowing of a germ, the implanting of a principle of spiritual life, and conversion is never so intelligible as where this fact is clearly recognized. There is life in the unrenewed Christian, even as there is life in the spawn or the egg; without this how could either ever grow to life under whatever warmth of the parent breast, or quickening rays of the sun? But what is a mere passive potential life, unkindled into active, conscious life? Thus with regard to baptized persons the question is not, 'Have they life?' but 'Are they alive?'

Dora Greenwell, *Two Friends*
(London: The Epworth Press, 1952), p. 78

The final area of women's self-understanding which would be studied and applied in a wider context was that of health care. Just as uncleanliness and impurity were linked in the voices which laid out their proper roles and duties for women, so too there was an identification of medical care with something old and primitive and therefore deeply complicated. Elizabeth Moberly Bell takes up the story.

In the eleventh century Salerno possessed the earliest medical school and its reputation stood high throughout Europe. There were women professors in the faculty and gradually the department for women's diseases was handed over entirely to women. Among the distinguished women professors was one called Trotula, whose books on gynaecology were studied for 500 years; Chaucer records that one of her books was in the library of the Wife of Bath. Throughout the ages, especially in times of peace, there were outbursts of hostility from the men, who wished to stop the women from practising. There was a pleasant tale of a period in the history of Athens, when a law was passed prohibiting the practice of medicine by women.

It would appear that a noble lady, horrified at the low standard of male practitioners, determined to defy the law and, disguised as a man, studied medicine and practised most successfully among women. Her disguise being penetrated, she was brought before the Areopagus and condemned to death. Whereupon the women who had been her patients invaded the court, threatening to abandon their homes and husbands unless the sentence was reversed and the law altered. This story, related by a celebrated midwife in James II's reign, has probably little foundation in fact, but the spirit behind the alleged law has expressed itself at frequent intervals. The Pope in 1341 made an Edict forbidding women to practise, and the Guild of English Surgeons in 1541 passed a Resolution 'that no carpenter, smith, weaver or woman practise surgery.' But the women were not stopped by Edict or Resolution. The sick came to them, and they served them as best they could. It was a risky business, for the death of a patient might well be followed by an accusation of witchcraft.

E. Moberly Bell, *Storming the Citadel: The Rise of the Woman Doctor*
(London: Constable & Co. Ltd, 1953), pp. 23–4

This chapter has examined three areas in which the aspirations of women placed them at an interface. As they began to listen to the authority of their own voices they were energized to seek for glory. Traditional roles were no longer enough; traditional activities, meanwhile, such as cooking, cleaning and caring for the sick, could be reclaimed. This meant moving into a dialogue which would change attitudes within the home, as this chapter has shown. But a further conversation awaited them if they were to change attitudes in Church and society.

CHAPTER 6

⁓

A MAGNIFICENT
WOMEN'S MEETING

'Sing to the Lord a new song, his praise in the assembly
of the faithful' (Psalm 149.1)

*Where the women hymn writers discovered theological literacy
and the preachers proclaimed a liberating word, the women
campaigners became activists for the divine economy. We have
seen already that the experience they brought to the task was
formidable. They had learned the lessons of their experience. They
could cook, clean and care. Now they would apply the same
determination which had driven them at home to tackling a wide-
ranging social agenda for change. Theirs would become an
increasingly prophetic as well as a pastoral voice.*

*So what drove the early campaigning activists? First, they
knew how to organize time. Well, one would of necessity when
accustomed to a working day such as this:*

Daily Work
Get up to prepare breakfast (7.15 a.m.).
Rouse children; serve husband's and own breakfast (7.45 a.m.).
Serve children's breakfast (8.15 a.m.).
Get children off to school (8.45 a.m.).
Turn down beds and open windows.
Clear away meals and wash up; clean up kitchen.
Dust and tidy living room and hall.
Make beds; tidy bedrooms and bathroom.
Do weekly work – see next List (finish by 11 a.m.).

Reading to the prisoners in gaol

Have your elevenses and a short rest; prepare yourself to go out
(11.30 a.m.).
Shopping (say 1 hour).
Have your own lunch and a longer rest.
Personal recreation – hobbies, gardening, visiting, etc.
(3.30 p.m.).
Prepare and serve tea (4.15 p.m.).
Prepare evening meal, tidy yourself, serve evening meal
(6.30 p.m.).
Clear up in kitchen and get children to bed (7.30 p.m.).
Relaxation, visiting, etc. (but special chores on Tuesday
and Wednesdays – see next List) until bedtime.

Carlton Wallace (ed.), *The Housewife's Pocket Book*
(London: Evans Brothers Ltd, 1953), p. 15

Carlton Wallace's programme is followed by a detailed examin-
ation of all these tasks. He is something of a tyrant where
housework is concerned and subtly patronizing when he genera-
lizes about the transferable skills which women won in the home.

RUNNING THE HOME

HOME MANAGEMENT is not an easy job, and unless a little thought
is given to organising, it can easily become sheer drudgery, with
everything in a muddle and the work never done.

A common rebuke to domestic servants in grandmother's day
was: 'Your head will never save your feet, my girl!' and in that
rebuke is the secret of avoiding drudgery. Just a little thought,
just a little planning, and a great deal of the hard work of running
a home can be eliminated.

Good home management depends mainly upon two things:
living within one's means, or Budgeting; and getting the work
done, or Household Routine.

Carlton Wallace (ed.), *The Housewife's Pocket Book*
(London: Evans Brothers Ltd, 1953), p. 1

We would use expressions such as resource and time management
to describe these skills. Women themselves used a more hard-

*headed approach to point out some of the snares which lurk in the
agenda of the over-dedicated. It is all very well to be told to have a
(short) rest. The deeper questions remain unaddressed. These are
about rights and duties, about who works anyway, about what
rest is and about what re-creates us.*

Maude Royden's is a particularly authoritative voice.

Please realise that a woman has as much right to work as a man,
and as much need to eat and drink. And I have some sympathy
with the speaker who said the other day – and I am glad to think
he was a man and not a woman – who said that there are
circumstances which make it almost a more tragic thing when a
woman is out of work than when a man is, for a woman, in spite of
the convenient assumption that she does not need to eat and drink
does need to eat and drink. And I sometimes think that if our
Lord were to ask her not, 'Why stand ye idle here all the day long?'
but 'Why do you walk the pavement of Piccadilly all the night
long?' she might reply, 'Because no man has hired me to do
anything better.' It is a kind of false sentiment which assumes that
women do not need to work. Everyone who has self-respect needs
to work and I do not think you will get a really efficient and
working scheme to deal with unemployment if you deliberately
ignore the claims of the women who are suffering as much today
from unemployment as the men.

A. Maude Royden, *Political Christianity*
(London: G. P. Putnam's Sons, 1922), pp. 50–1

*Leonora Eyles also picks up the theme of gender and expectations
in her analysis.*

Another internal disability against which some women labour is
their inborn habit of taking too much on their own shoulders. The
married woman with a job uncomplainingly and cheerfully sets
off to her daily work often after a night spent in nursing a husband
or a sick child, and a few hours wrestling with the incompetent
maids of today, or of doing her own work unaided. No man would
attempt such a thing. The widower left with a family immediately

gets a housekeeper or another wife, and the state of a home left temporarily without a mother during illness or holiday shows what an amazing amount of usually unnoticed work and organisation a woman must get through in the course of a day; in fact, the more effectively she does her work, the less she is appreciated, because household tasks are not noticed until they are done badly or left undone.

If women are to enter the market in competition with men, they will have to conserve their energies much more than they do at present.

Leonora Eyles, *Careers for Women*
(London: Elkin Mathews & Marrot, 1930), pp. 26–7

Conserving energy is a much more sophisticated concept than simply taking a short rest before tackling the next task. Maude Royden's 'twopenn'orth of dark' has its present-day equivalents.

When the war was over, and the women had gone back to their 'own' work, it was found that some of them had conceived such an appetite for leisure that they had actually been seen sitting down and reading a newspaper. I shall never forget the horror on the faces of those who reported to me this unexpected sight.

Yet, especially now that women are voters, it might have been hailed as a good omen that they should occasionally read a newspaper? Or if it must be assumed by the sort of critics who always take a gloomy view of human nature that the women were merely reading the abysmal idiocies that appear on the 'Woman's Page', at least the spectacle of a woman sitting down to do it need not have seemed more shocking than a man doing so to read the betting news? It did, however, shock observers to the core.

So quite a lot of women pay sixpence and sit in a cinema. It is warm in there, and the seat is comfortable; but best of all, it is dark and no one will see that they are women sitting down.

In the old days, when the cinema was cheaper even than now, young people used to speak of having 'twopenn'orth of dark'. The phrase aroused suspicion in the minds of women; even so, the purpose of the suspected ones was not so nefarious as that of the woman who wanted nothing more than a seat and gladly paid twopence for it – in the dark.

A. Maude Royden, *Women's Partnership in the New World*
(London: George Allen & Unwin Ltd, 1941), pp. 92–3

Hers is a religious and spiritual commentary, for she realizes that the root problem is guilt.

You cannot give that extra half-hour or hour to work. You must give it to some relaxation; you must go to some perfectly idiotic cinema (they are not all idiotic, I do not mean that) because your temper and body and mind are all tired. Well, then, do it and do it deliberately and do it with your eyes open. You cannot give that extra bit of time because you are too tired. Well, then, you are too tired: recognise the fact and thank God there is a silly cinema you can go to. And in doing this, do it with your eyes open and do not do it with that sense of half guilt, with that ashamed feeling that you ought to have if you were doing something weak or wrong. You cannot help it: you must read that detective story, you must do something that makes no demand on your moral or intellectual or physical strength. You must, and yet while you know that you must, you still have, haven't you, a slightly guilty sense about it? You wonder whether perhaps you ought not really to be doing something better, although you do not mean to do that something better!

Get rid of that sense. Look at it quite clearly. Is it really a need of your physical and mental being that you get some mental relaxation? Well, if it is, take it, and for God's sake do not get an uneasy conscience about it, because an uneasy conscience is a disease that it takes a very clever doctor to cure.

A. Maude Royden, *Here and Hereafter*
(London: Putnam, 1933), p. 23

Mrs Harding Wood's comforting book, Women – Are You Listening? *also picks up an important issue. For her assumption is that women may not want to rest alone. What they seek is company.*

Mothers and home-makers work so hard and they often get dreadfully tired. Your back aches, and your feet! You just long for an hour's rest: How welcome the Women's Fellowship is where you can come and sit and rest and enjoy a cup of tea and a friendly chat – and then enter into the helpful meeting which follows joining in the hymns, learning week by week 'what a privilege to carry everything to God in Prayer', and listening to the message which the Leader has brought from the Word of God to cheer you, teach you, encourage, help and strengthen you in your daily lives. She will tell you of the Rest of conscience and the peace of heart under all circumstances which you will have when you open the door of your heart and admit the Saviour who is knocking so patiently.

Something else He brings too, and that is the gift of true joy.

Mrs G. R. Harding Wood, *Women – Are You Listening?*
(London: Lutterworth Press, 1954), pp. 134–5

It should be added that resource management too came up for fierce scrutiny.

Now for the pies. I never see an apple-pie without thinking of the sad waste of time and labour and substances of which it is the outcome. To put that king of fruits, the apple, all shaven and shorn of its gorgeous covering and the wealth of flavour and fragrance and bone food that go with it, into a foul, pasty mass of hogs' lard and starch, is for me the literal rendering of the wise man's 'jewel in a swine's snout'.

Mary J. Studley, *What Our Girls Ought to Know*
(New York: Holbrook & Co., 1881), p. 47

Fifty years later, Lillian and Arthur Horth's text is far less exiting, though it makes the all-important connection between cooking and cleaning up after you.

If you are tiny girlies, ask Mother or an elder sister to separate the yolk from the white of egg as the yolk will not be needed, and perhaps they will blanch the almonds for you as well, then you should be able to get along with yourself.

It is a jolly game if you are allowed to have a little friend in the kitchen to help you. If you put away everything tidily afterwards and leave all the things you have used washed up, you are sure to get permission.

Lillian B. and Arthur C. Horth, *101 Things for Girls to Do:*
Being a Review of Simple Crafts and Household Subjects
(London: B. T. Batsford Ltd, 1932), pp. 135–6

With nurturing goes a quest for purity. And this is where the campaigning women really came into their own. They invented social purity. That is to say that women organized themselves for change. Inspired by a great vision of what might be, as opposed to what presently was, they tackled social problems such as alcoholism and its effects upon the home, the exploitation of prostitutes, and taboos surrounding dress and clothing.

Mrs Harding Wood's description of the Women's Fellowship may have sounded anodyne, but we would be quite mistaken if we were to forget that the oldest of our women's Church organizations were highly politicized.

Now our women's organisations give us far more power than we have as individuals to attack great, social evils, to stand as battalions where the Son of God goes forth to war. What needs doing here, that this band of women can collectively try to do? What about the children and their needs? And when our collective effort is decided upon, what help can we get from our own men folk, who should stand shoulder to shoulder with us if our cause is a righteous one? And let us never forget that every organisation of Christian women gains a special strength from reliance on the Master's own promise. 'If two of You shall agree on earth as touching anything that they shall ask, it shall be done for them of My Father.' Subject, of course, to the great condition that what we ask is not against His will, it SHALL be done. Not all at once, perhaps, not as we should like it done, perhaps, but still it shall be done because we ask. And if we ask in any sort of sincerity we cannot fail to try to bring about the good thing we ask for, in our service to our neighbours. 'Come thou with us and we will seek to do thee good,' said the woman of Israel long ago. It is surely our own ideal that we must share, nothing less than that.

Mrs E. M. Field, *Addresses to Mothers*
(London: James Clarke & Co. Ltd, 1926), p. 173

Frances Willard organized the Women's Temperance Union of Chicago. She would become celebrated as an educator and be appointed the first President of the Evanston College for Ladies.

But American womanhood had awakened from sleep, and had begun to realise the power which lay within its reach. It had awakened too, effectually, to a consciousness of the evil which was sapping the strength of the nation, was undermining its moral nature, and invading the sanctity of its home life. And, realising these things, it understood that the time for inaction was for ever past, that a firm stand must be made, and made without delay, if this evil was to be overcome. The cry of suffering and sinning humanity had ascended to heaven, and each woman in that great Temperance Army felt that a divine commission rested upon her to

'Charge for the God of battles
And put the foe to rout.'

W. J. Wintle and Florence Witts, *Florence Nightingale and Frances E. Willard: The Story of Their Lives*
(London: Sunday School Union, n.d.), p. 65

The God of battles is also invoked in this fiery writing from Millicent Fawcett's account of a meeting convened by Josephine Butler and those who campaigned on behalf of 'the new teaching and revolt of women'. That is to say, who opposed the provisions of the Contagious Diseases Act.

On a certain afternoon, when Mr. Childers, the Government candidate, was again to address a large meeting from the window of a house, I and my lady friends determined to hold a meeting at the same hour, thinking we should be unmolested. We had to go all over the town before we found anyone bold enough to let us a place to meet in. At last, we found a large hayloft over an empty room on the outskirts of the town. You could only ascent to it by means of a kind of ladder, leading through a trap-door in the floor. However, the place was large enough to hold a good meeting, and soon filled. Stuart had run on in advance and paid for the room in his own name, and looked in to see that all was right. He found the floor strewn with cayenne pepper to make it impossible for us to speak, and there were some bundles of straw in the empty room below. He got a poor woman to help him and with buckets of water he managed to drench the floor and sweep together the cayenne pepper. Still, when we arrived, it was very unpleasant for eyes and throat. We began our meeting with prayer, and the women were listening with increasing determination never to forsake the good cause, when a smell of burning was felt, smoke began to curl up through the floor, and a threatening noise was then heard underneath at the door. The bundles of straw beneath had been set on fire, and the smoke much annoyed us. To our horror, looking down the room to the trap-door entrance, we saw head after head appear; man after man came in, until they crowded the place. There was no possible exit for us, the windows being high above the ground, and we were gathered into one end of the room like a flock of sheep surrounded by wolves. They were mostly *not* Yorkshire people; they were led on by two or three *gentlemen (?)* one of them became afterwards a candidate for Parliament.

It would hardly do to describe in words what followed. It was a time which required strong faith and calm courage. Mrs. Wilson and I stood in front of the company of women, side by side. She whispered in my ear: 'Now is the time to trust in God; don't let us fear.' And a wonderful sense of the Divine presence came to us both. You understand, it was not so much personal violence that we feared, as what would have been to any of us worse than death; for the indecencies of the men, their gestures and threats, were what I would prefer not to describe. Their language was hideous. They shook their fists in our faces, with volleys of oaths. This continued for some time, and we had no defence or means of escape. Their chief rage was directed against me; half a dozen fists were in my face at once, and the epithets applied were such as one only hears of in brothels. They filled their foul talk with allusions to the 'visites' under the Contagious Diseases Acts, with which they all seemed minutely familiar. It was very clear that they understood that 'their craft was in danger.' The new teaching and revolt of women had stirred up the very depths of hell. We said nothing, for our voices could not have been heard. We simply stood shoulder to shoulder – Mrs. Wilson and I – and waited and endured. But it seemed all the time as if some strong angel were present, for when these men's hands were literally upon us, they seemed held back by some unseen power. There was a young Yorkshire woman, strong and stalwart, with bare arms, and a shawl over her head, among our flock behind us. She dashed forward and fought her way through the crowd of men, and escaped down the ladder, and running as hard as she could, she found Mr. Stuart on the outskirts of Mr. Childers' meeting, and said to him: 'Come! Run! they are killing Mrs. Butler.' He did run and came up the ladder stairs into the midst of the crowd. As soon as they perceived that he was our defender, they were down on him. A strong man seized him in his arms; another opened the window, and they were going to throw him headlong out. I ran forward between him and the window. This was enough to give him time to slip cleverly from between the man's arms on to the floor and glide away to the side where we were. He then asked to be allowed to say a few words to them, and with good temper and coolness, he argued that he had taken the room, that it was his, and if they would kindly let the ladies go, he would hear what they had to say. A fierce argument began. Meanwhile, stones were thrown into the windows, and broken glass flew across the room. While all this was going on (it seemed to us like hours of horrible endurance), hope came at last, in the shape of two or three helmeted policemen, whose heads appeared one by one up through the trap-door. Now, we thought, we are safe! But no! These Metropolitans had been hired by the Government, and

87

they simply looked at the scene for a few moments with a cynical smile, and left the place without an attempt to defend us. My heart grew sick as I saw them disappear. It seemed now to become desperate.

Mrs. Wilson and I whispered to each other in the midst of the din: 'let us ask God to help us, and make a rush for the entrance.' Two or three Yorkshire working women put themselves in the front, and we pushed our way I don't know how to the stairs. It was only myself and one or two other ladies that the men really cared to do violence to; so if we could get away, the rest would be alright. I made a dash forward and took one flying leap from the trap door onto the ground floor below. It was a long jump, but, being light, I came down all right. I was not a bit too soon, for the feet of the men were ready to kick my head as it disappeared down the hole. I found Mrs. Wilson after me very soon in the street. Once in the street, of course, these cowards did not dare to offer us the same violence. We went straight to our own hotel, and there we had a magnificent women's meeting. Such a revulsion of feeling came over the inhabitants of Pontefract when they heard of this disgraceful scene, that they flocked to hear us, many of the women weeping. We had to turn the lights low, and close the windows for fear of the mob; but the hotel was literally crowded with women, and we scarcely needed to speak – events had spoken for us and all honest hearts were won.

Millicent G. Fawcett and E. M. Turner, *Josephine Butler*
(London: The Association for Moral and Social Hygiene, 1927), pp. 81–5

Thirty years after this account was written, Kathleen Bliss would still be making theological connections. In the home women had learned how to clean. They had also learned what was clean and what was not. When they moved out of the home to campaign, this knowledge gave them, corporately and as individuals, an enormous power and freedom to work for true purity.

Though few would admit as much, many Christians believe that the woman is a secondary being, an agent enabling and completing man: probing will uncover the existence of ancient taboos about women's impurity, still lurking in most unexpected places. Many of the women who have written in the reports quoted in this book feel a sense of despair about the way in which Bible texts are used to justify and support already held opinions about the place of women in the Church. When Churches are in a desperate position for lack of man-power, all sorts of service is gladly accepted from women: when the situation is eased, theological reasons against women doing this kind of work are at once raised. Some women feel quite as strongly the debasement of theology involved in this procedure as true injustice to women. Other reports speak of gifted women who have gained qualifications in divinity, for whom the Church finds no place. Very many reports refer to the low pay and status accorded to full time women workers in the Church and to the uncertainty which surrounds their position.

Kathleen Bliss, *The Service and Status of Women in the Churches*
(London: SCM Press Ltd, 1952), p. 198

Caroline Adams, writing six years later, would write the 'mission statement' of the social purity campaigners: 'The nature of true virginity is not determined at the physical level.'

The other phrase concerning our Lady, 'Ever-Virgin' was endorsed by the fifth General Council of the Church in A.D. 553. The English Church sits light to this Council, but the term Virgin has been present in the Creeds from the beginning, no less than in the Bible. The concept of virginity is so repugnant to some Protestant thought on occasion it almost seems to rank with unnatural vice. This deep-seated, even if unrecognized, inhibition is responsible for much defective Christology, for virginity alone could make possible Mary's motherhood. Unless virgin, and ever-virgin, the child she bore could not have been God. The nature of true virginity is not determined at the physical level, which is rather the outcome of the virgin spirit than virginity itself. We disallow the undeviating, steady stream of enshrined Spirit-guided tradition at the peril of dissociating ourselves from our source.

Caroline Adams, *Articles of Thy Belief*
(London: SPCK, 1958), pp. 44–5

Dorothy L. Sayers would also lean on its insights with her own caustic moral message. Hers is a challenging voice to the churches, a timely reminder that women who speak out will, of necessity, be unpopular.

The Church says Covetousness is a deadly sin – but does she really think so? Is she ready to found Welfare Societies to deal with financial immorality as she does with sexual immorality? Do the officials stationed at church doors in Italy to exclude women with bare arms turn anybody away on the grounds that they are too well-dressed to be honest? Do the vigilance committees who complain of 'suggestive' books and plays make any attempt to suppress the literature which 'suggests' that getting on in the world is the only object in life? Is Dives, like Magdalen, ever refused the sacraments on the grounds that he, like her, is an 'open and notorious evil-liver'? Does the Church arrange services with bright congregational singing for Total Abstainers from Usury?

The Church's record is not, in these matters, quite as good as it might be. But is perhaps rather better than that of those who denounce her for her neglect. The Church is not the Vatican, nor the Metropolitans, nor the Bench of Bishops; it is not even the Vicar or the Curate or the Church wardens: the Church is you and I. And are you and I in the least sincere in our pretence that we disapprove of Covetousness?

Dorothy L. Sayers, *Creed or Chaos?*
(London: Methuen & Co. Ltd, 1947), p. 76

Now Dorothy Sayers was a great campaigner for freedom of dress for women. No wonder that this theme, too, runs through a number of the writings of the moral hygienists.

In every sense of the word Miss Willard was a strict hygienist, and looked forward hopefully to the time when women's dress would become less of a restraint and weariness, when custom would cease to impose grievous burdens upon the so-called weaker sex, and when simple natural habits, coupled with pure, plain food and a reasonable costume, would ensure the sound body which alone can prove the fitting complement of the sound mind.

W. J. Wintle and Florence Witts, *Florence Nightingale
and Frances E. Willard: The Story of Their Lives*
(London: Sunday School Union, n.d.), pp. 134–5

*There is a further link here. What constitutes a 'sound body' and a
'sound mind'? The third area of human experience which women
had learned in the home and which they now came to question in
the public domain was the issue of health care. The Catholic
mystic Caryll Houselander describes a hospital visit.*

I had an incredible day at the Lunatic Asylum yesterday. Met several Queens – Female ones – one the 'Queen of the Whole Earth' whose hand I was allowed to kiss and who conferred many titles upon me. Half, more than half, the lunatics are practically sane, except on one point, and some even go out to work every day. I've seldom – if ever – been present at anything so moving as the prayers in the tiny Catholic chapel in the evening, organized entirely by the patients, the prayers of their own choosing and said aloud; and what a mystery and what an example – an ex-Trappist monk, a young girl, an old lady bent double nearly, but in spite of it and of being insane, beautiful, and a handful of others, all people who had started out in life intent on a high vocation, and given it indeed utter abnegation, put away in a lunatic asylum: and this is the point – they reached out in their prayers to the whole world. As I knelt among them listening at first and in the end joining in unconsciously with them, I grew more and more amazed at their petitions:
'For Russia'
'For the suffering people of Europe'
'For the starving people of India'

'For the sick'
'For prisoners'
'For the conversion of the world'
'For purity of heart in the world'
'For purity of heart here.'

And then, to me the most moving petition of all, 'That we here in this little chapel dedicated to Your Divine Heart may have perfect abandonment to Your dear will.'

Maisie Ward, *Caryll Houselander: That Divine Eccentric*
(London: Sheed & Ward, 1962), pp. 269–70

Her biographer, Maisie Ward, notes of Houselander that

Works of sheer spirituality have very seldom been written by the laity, and we must go back far indeed to find an English Catholic laywoman writing one. Dame Julian of Norwich won for her book the right to stand beside those of Benedictine, Carmelite or Trappist. Priests from many orders welcomed Caryll Houselander instantly, recognizing that she was precisely not 'just another' spiritual writer. She has occasional echoes of Julian, whose Revelations she loved. But the element which will, I think, make *The Comforting of Christ*, *The Reed of God*, *The Flowering Tree*, and above all *Guilt* permanently important was very different and totally her own.

Like Julian she was looking towards God, praying to Him, telling of Him; but the medieval did not think so much about the individual character of those who must be led also to look, also to pray. What she wrote had been given to her as revelation experienced, it was not the fruit of her own contact with her fellow-sinners. Caryll Houselander had a very unusual insight into individual character, quite distinct from her insight into divine revelation, though woven into one vision with it. She could see what was there in the people she wanted to help, and she could say what she saw.

Part of what Monsignor Knox welcomed in her freshness of approach to the oldest of doctrines came from an intense realism about human nature. St. John tells us that Our Lord would not trust Himself to men 'because He knew what was in man.' Yet the overwhelming fact was to follow that at the Last Supper He gave Himself into the hands of men, said to them, 'I am in My Father, and you in Me, and I in you': one of those to whom He said it was about to deny Him. And the risen Christ said to St. Paul, who was persecuting His followers, 'Saul, Saul, why persecutest thou Me?'

Maisie Ward, *Caryll Houselander: That Divine Eccentric*
(London: Sheed & Ward, 1962), p. 5

The same sense of community with the persecuted inspires Maude Royden to write,

Recently there has been a considerable agitation about the way in which the mentally unsound are treated in our asylums. I do not propose to dwell at length on the worst of these accusations. They range from mere indifference to actually brutal and horrible treatment. But it is extraordinarily difficult for anyone who is in no sense an expert to vouch for the truth of any one particular statement. What, however, is to me rather terrible is the unanimity of these accusations. I am told on good medical authority that the memory of a patient who has been out of his mind, but is now sound again, is quite as trustworthy as that of any person who has never been deranged. Therefore one must not dismiss his complaints as the complaints of one who can have no clear recollection of what happened to him. And when we get so great a body of evidence so strikingly alike from people quite independent of one another, not from the same asylum, and not knowing the evidence each has given, evidence both from attendants and from the patients themselves, I cannot resist the belief that there is an indubitable case for the closest inquiry. Well, what ought we to demand? We ought to demand that the system under which the mentally deranged are bound to come should be more open to the day, more deliberate in its operation, more scrupulously and meticulously careful of the rights of these most helpless people, than perhaps any other system dealing with any other section of the community.

A. Maude Royden, *Political Christianity*
(London: G. P. Putnam's Sons, 1922), p. 133

The most famous nurse of all was Edith Cavell. She took her place 'standing in the view of God and Eternity' before going to her execution.

It was past 9.30 (German time); Edith Cavell had given up hope of seeing the Chaplain, but on being told that he had come, she put on her dressing-gown and was ready in a few moments. Stirling Gahan wrote an account of how he found her.

'The warder opened the cell door and there stood my friend. On my way to the prison I had been apprehensive as to the condition of mind in which I might find her. Distraught? Bitter? Unnerved? Full of hopeless grief? but all anxieties were set at rest in a moment. There she stood, her bright, gentle, cheerful self; as always, quietly smiling, calm and collected. She seemed well in body; quiet in mind and even cheerful and gave me a kind and grateful welcome.'

Edith Cavell smiled, shook hands with Stirling Gahan, gestured to him to sit down on the wooden chair, then – mistress of meiosis to the last – observed, 'It is good of you to come.' Stirling Gahan noticed the forlorn and faded flowers that her nurses had been allowed to bring her nearly a month before (she had acknowledged the gift in her letter of September 25). The cell was clean and sparsely comfortable. They stood for some time talking. 'Miss Cavell said that she expected it would end thus – her trial had been fairly conducted, and her sentence what, under the circumstances, she had expected. She was thankful to God for the absolute quiet of her ten weeks' imprisonment. It had been like a solemn fast from all earthly distractions and diversions.'

Some time during this period they sat down, she on the bed and Stirling Gahan on the wooden chair.

'I have no fear nor shrinking,' she said. 'I have seen death so often that it is not strange or fearful to me . . . life has always been hurried and full of difficulty. This time of rest has been a great mercy. Everyone here has been very kind.' Then quietly and clearly she gave her message to the world.

'This I would say, standing as I do in view of God and Eternity, I realize that patriotism is not enough: I must have no hatred or bitterness towards anyone.'

'There was no moveable table in the cell,' wrote Stirling Gahan, 'but we sat upon the edge of the bed with the one chair between us. This served as our Communion table, and I placed the vessels, with the bread and wine, upon it. Then we partook of the Lord's Supper together, and she evidently felt deeply the sweet and solemn service. After the Blessing, we remained for a moment silently in prayer, then I began softly to repeat the words of "Abide with Me". At first in a whisper, but soon quite clearly she united with me in the sacred words, and so we repeated together that beautiful hymn of prayer and praise.

'Afterwards she spoke of her sinfulness and unworthiness. How could she be sure that heaven was for her after death? I told the story of the thief on the Cross, with the Saviour's assuring words "today shalt thou be with me in paradise". Jesus was almighty to forgive and to save, and to admit all his pardoned ones into his Blessed Presence and Rest. This covered all the need and ended all anxiety.'

During the final conversation when she sent farewell messages to friends and relations, Stirling Gahan is reported to have said, 'We shall always remember you as a heroine and as a martyr,' occasioning the reply, 'Don't think of me like that; think of me only as a nurse who tried to do her duty.'

Rowland Ryder, Edith Cavell
(London: Book Club Edition, 1975), pp. 213–14

In 1912, Mrs Holmes had written an impassioned piece on the spirituality of the 'communicant-nurse'.

By the constitutions of the Guild, it is required of every member that she must be a Communicant of the Church of England. She must honestly believe that the 'Church of England' is 'The Church' in England. Believing this, she will be enthusiastic for her Church. And she will show forth this enthusiasm in the exercise of her Profession. And this, perhaps, in two ways: – she will, when possible, secure the Sacrament of Baptism for the children, and the Blessed Sacrament for the sick and dying. It is in Baptism that the children are safely placed in the Arms of the great Child-Lover. 'It is certain,' says the Prayer Book, 'that children which are Baptized, dying before they commit actual sin, are undoubtedly saved.' The Church does not say that a child dying unbaptized is undoubtedly lost. What the Church does say is, that a child dying after it is baptized, and before it commits wilful sin, is undoubtedly saved. And you may be the means of securing this 'undoubted certainty' for the child: you – the Nurse, and often no one but the Nurse – may get permission to send for a Priest; you – if the child is dying and no Priest can be had – may yourself baptize it with water, in the Name of the Blessed Trinity. Happy Nurse! to be able, as a Nurse, in the exercise of her profession, to secure the 'undoubted certainty' of a little one's salvation. So, too, with the Blessed Sacrament. 'She must be a Communicant.' Why? Surely because 'The Body of our Lord Jesus Christ', dwelling in her, alone can fill her heart with that permanent sense of the sacredness of the human body which Nurses so easily lose. It is the Communicant-Nurse who best can realise 'who visit the sick, visit Christ; who touch their wounds, touch His'. It is the Communicant who best can hear Him whisper over each patient, 'Behold My hands and My feet, that it is I Myself; you are tending Me.' Yes! 'She must be a Communicant,' because the Chalice is the true well – and 'the well is deep' – from whence she can ever draw the life-gladdening enthusiasm which no routine and no unloveliness can kill. 'She must be a Communicant,' because the only work fit to be offered on the Altar is work which has come from the Altar. 'She must be a Communicant,' and if she is a Communicant herself she will long with a great longing to secure the Communion for the Sick and Dying. This is her privilege – that she, and often no one else, can suggest and provide for a soul a 'provision by the way'. Happy Nurse! to be able, as a Nurse, in the exercise of her profession, to secure the last Sacrament for a soul as it passes out of that body which she has tended. 'She must be a Communicant.' So will the glow from her own Communions be communicated to others; and they too will catch enthusiasm of her burning heart – of 'God in' her.

E. E. Holmes, *In Watchings Often*
(London: Longman, Green & Co., 1912), pp. 196–8

This passionate voice is matched by a prophetic one. In this concluding extract Elizabeth Moberly Bell puts into words what many women already knew:

In that future men and women working together in the medical profession face a task of immense complexity. In the modern conception of medicine it is not merely the science of healing but also the whole art of healthy living for which the nation looks to its doctors for guidance. The problems of health do not grow simpler in a community, largely urban, living in overcrowded and often insanitary conditions, in an age when moral restraints are little thought of. They are problems which demand for their solution the highest qualities of brain and character. It is well that energy is no longer to be dissipated in a fruitless struggle between the sexes.

E. Moberly Bell, *Storming the Citadel: The Rise of the Woman Doctor*
(London: Constable & Co. Ltd, 1953), p. 191

CHAPTER 7

~~

A HIGH HONOUR AND A
PRESSING DUTY

'The power of the Most High will overshadow you' (Luke 1.35)

The call to action which women first heard in their own homes and then voiced in the outer world of their social concerns was mirrored by another call. This call was addressed to their very sense of identity. It would lead them to question their status within the human and divine plan; it would lead them to seek the vote and thence ordination to priesthood. This chapter sets out the ingredients to this quest for a distinctive identity; the next will explore how it worked out in practice.

But as Miss Nightingale paced through the autumn woods, where once she used to make friends with the squirrels and the birds, she felt that a duty was laid upon her. She began to see the meaning of the strange impulse which first led her to take up the work of nursing. Her experiences at Kaiserwerth, with the sisters of St. Vincent de Paul at Paris, and in the Home at Harley Street, now took shape as a qualification for a harder but grander work.

It was the call of God. She heard the Voice – to hear which is both a high honour and a pressing duty – the Voice which the servants of God have ever been quick to recognise; and it seemed to say, 'Whom shall I send, and who will go for ME?'

There was no hesitation. Florence Nightingale had learned to

Florence Nightingale in her travelling carriage at the seat of war

obey. Right from her woman's heart the answer came, 'Here am I; send me.'

W. J. Wintle and Florence Witts,
Florence Nightingale and Frances E. Willard: The Story of Their Lives
(London: Sunday School Union, n.d.), p. 48

The biographers of Florence Nightingale and Frances Willard use scriptural vocabulary to describe the call to obedience. The divine purpose is made known to an individual. Her task is to answer in faith. This constitutes her obedience. Now the call in this, and many other cases, is not mediated through a series of relationships. Its context may be the home, but also, equally easily, it could be 'the autumn woods'. Here the woman in question would not be seen as wife, daughter or mother; she would be like the Virgin Mary at the moment of the incarnation, standing alone before God.

This could be an isolating experience. Indeed it still is to many women pioneers. When we examine the ways in which the women in this chapter first heard and lived in obedience to the call of God, then we can isolate certain trends which are still applicable. Young women who sought for identity and a new sense of purpose were not supported by the frank and friendly voices which egged on their brothers.

Give me your hand, my dear young friend, and I will lead you to the dark passages and the rugged steeps whose forbidding shadows fall gloomily on the highway of life. I will also conduct you to the green and sunny spots whereon you may indulge in innocent delights. Open your heart to my counsels! I will teach you how to escape the teeming dangers, which, like troops of ill-omened phantoms, wait in the 'slippery places' of youth, seeking his destruction. I will unload to you the secrets of success and of eminence in this life, and the sure means of winning a crown of glory in the next!

It is, without doubt, a very joyous thought to you, that you have become a young man. Manhood has long been the fairy land of your boyhood's reverie.

Your full heart swells, as you exclaim:

> 'Time on my brow hath set his seal;
> I start to find myself a man.'

Daniel Wise, *The Young Man's Counsellor: or Sketches and Illustrations of the Duties and Dangers of Young Men* (London: Yorkshire J. S. Publishing and Stationery Co. Ltd, n.d.), pp. 13–14

So who was there to 'give a hand' by unloading the 'secrets of success' on to the young women? In what sense were they offered any encouragement for their journey into humanity? This was a theological task of considerable importance, as Sister Emily realized.

It is difficult to persuade any woman to go wrong if she is a Christian, for religion is a safeguard fixed between God and mankind by the power of God and the worship that men and women pay to God. I have read many books of advice to sons, but none to the daughters, so my desire in writing this is to protect young girls by unveiling the covert designs too frequently lurking in the breasts of many lustful men, which end in the destruction of unsuspecting maidenhood.

Sister Emily, *Was Eve Guilty?*
(London: Messrs Hill, Cook & Lane, n.d.), p. 11

Women needed a past; they needed role models; they needed a new understanding of what they could be and become. This is why the exploratory work of the women church historians is so important. They discovered a glorious 'past' for the women's movement. Lina Eckenstein is one of the great luminaries of church history writing. She wrote quite unselfconsciously, long before feminist history became fashionable.

We have seen women ministering to Christ and the Apostles; we have seen them adopting the garb and appearance of a man in order to go forth and devote themselves to the cure of body and soul; we have seen them throwing open their houses as places of meeting, thereby contributing to the number of possible churches.

There was also the woman prophet, eager to add to the sum of revealed truth, cultivating visionary powers whereby she could feel herself in contact with powers that are divine. We have seen others devoted to the more practical work of collecting round them maidens whom they trained to habits of piety and industry, notably at the great settlement near Seleucia, associated with the name of Thecla. Settlements where, under the rule of a woman, the inmates combined devotion with the giving of medicinal help and well-considered advice.

We have watched the eagerness of women to teach the faith, and, finally, have seen the glory of the martyrs, that set the final seal on the new faith.

These possibilities were not carried forward in an uninter-rupted sequence. A time came when the Church had no place for the unmarried woman and when her needs and capacities were ignored. In the Church's estimation, the woman, socially, mor-ally and intellectually, was no more than the helpmate of man.

As history shows in other cases, a later age took up what seemed to have been wilfully cast aside, and the life of women in convents of their own, carried forward many of the neglected possibilities in a way beneficial to mankind. In the double monastery of Hilda of Whitby, in the Latin writing of Hrotsvitha (or Roswitha) of Saxony, in the philanthropy of Margaret of Scotland and of Agnes of Bohemia, in the great *Materia Medica* of St. Hildegard, we see brought to fruition the seeds of a much earlier sowing.

The cultivation of interests, devotional, intellectual, artistic, economic, medicinal, made the glory of the medieval convent. In this sense the life of women under monasticism is prepared for and heralded by the life of women under early Christianity.

Lina Eckenstein, *The Women of Early Christianity*
(London: The Faith Press, 1935), pp. 154–5

She wrote about women in the early Church and the great women religious of the medieval period. Her concern was to tell their story but also to examine what their contribution to church and social

*life had been. 'If they could do, then so can we' is the unspoken
subtext that runs throughout her major works. She rediscovered
evidence which had lain submerged in the Christian imagination.*

Women were allowed to prophesy in the Jewish Church, where
the belief held good that to speak under divine inspiration was
possible. This belief was carried on to the Christian era and some
of the first women prophets mentioned are the daughters of Philip
the evangelist, or deacon, called by these names in distinction to
Philip the Apostle.

These daughters are repeatedly mentioned by later writers.
They were, Hermione, Charitine, Irais and Eutyches, or Eutyc-
hiane. Chief among them was Hermione of whom the *Acta
Sanctorum* gives an account. Early in her life she and Eutyches
made a journey to Ephesus in Asia Minor, with intent to do
homage to John the Theologian who, however, they found to
have died.

Hermione settled in Ephesus and gave herself up to the practice
of medicine, numbers of people coming to be healed. But the
Emperor Trajan (97–117), on his way to Persia, was informed of
her faith and work and cited her before his tribunal. She bravely
bore the ordeal of scourging and, shamed, the Emperor set her
free. She then opened a public hospice and 'gave to all both bodily
and spiritual comfort'. At the beginning of Hadrian's reign she
was again called upon to give up her religion, and on refusing to
do so, suffered the extreme penalty after having converted her
executioners.

Lina Eckenstein, *The Women of Early Christianity*
(London: The Faith Press, 1935), pp. 128–9

*Among those who would take this inspiration to heart were the
pioneers of women's education. After all, in Eckenstein's writings
women are identified as teachers, preachers, martyrs, saints,
ministers of the gospel. In the next passage, from the life of Frances
Mary Buss and Dorothea Beale, we see that historical 'rescue
work' in fact served a wider cause. It provided the nineteenth-
century pioneers with role models.*

St Hilda, Abbess of Whitby, patroness of poetry and learning, 'whose example', said the Venerable Bede, 'afforded in her own day occasion of amendment and salvation to many who lived at a distance', was very real to Dorothea. She could see her own half-hidden aspiration flowering in this woman of royal descent, who 'lived for thirty-three years most nobly a secular life. Then, wishing to forsake all that she had for our Lord, (was) consecrated, and set over a special house by Bishop Aidan'. 'We read', wrote Dorothea in the College Magazine in 1886, 'that "for her singular piety and grace, all who knew her called her mother".' Like St Hilda, Dorothea was an earnest student. She, too, was the head of a great teaching establishment. And in St Hilda Dorothea saw the foreshadowing of her wish to be the founder, ruler and mother of 'a body of women whose one desire is to consecrate themselves to this ministry of teaching'.

Dorothea honoured the Saintly Abbess by naming after her three of the *parerga*, the additional works which arose from the College foundation. These were St Hilda's, Cheltenham, a residential training college for secondary women teachers; St Hilda's Hall (now College), which was founded in close connection with the first St Hilda's; and St Hilda's in the East, a settlement in East London, inaugurated, financed and largely run by old pupils of the Ladies' College.

To be called 'mother' in the sense that St Hilda was called mother was one of Dorothea's deepest desires. Where Frances Mary Buss gave vent to her maternal feelings with an enveloping hug and a kiss, Dorothea's expression was both more withdrawn and more intense. The outward expression was no more than the pressure of a hand, a deepening tone of voice, a sudden look of understanding in the all-seeing eyes.

Josephine Kamm, *How Different from Us: A Biography of Miss Buss and Miss Beale* (London: The Bodley Head, 1958), p. 121

Miss Beale would be one of many women who gained a sense of belonging to a tradition as a result of this archaeological work into the hidden history of women.

The Western Church gave tardy and grudging recognition to the Deaconess. Forms for their ordination are to be found in Italy and Gaul, but there are also canons of Councils forbidding them to be ordained. As has been pointed out, there were two tendencies at work, 'the one recognising the Deaconess and giving to her and other women definite parts in the administration of the sacraments and services of the Church, the other ignoring the Deaconess, or curtailing her position and limiting to the minimum the share of women in church services.' Such a clash of opinion is not peculiar to one era of Church history, but has been characteristic of its whole course, and indeed of every phase of the women's movement.

When the special circumstances which had called for the work of a Deaconess disappeared, she became merged in the nun. Women members of the Religious Orders were consecrated persons, bound by the life-long vows of poverty, chastity and obedience. While they had chaplains to say Mass, they themselves performed the full choir services, even when priests were present. In the seventh century, the golden age of English monasticism, nuns shared with monks in the work of the mission-field. St. Walburga and thirty companions, for example, went out from the Abbey of Wimborne to assist St. Boniface in the evangelization of Germany. In the late Middle Ages, nuns were more strictly confined to their convents. Here they embroidered vestments, fed and clothed the poor, provided schools for the daughters of the nobility and homes for single women. Such activities were auxiliary to their chief function, the performance of the *Opus Dei* or daily round of prayer and praise which they offered to God on behalf of all mankind.

Besides professed nuns there were secular canonesses, who were bound by the triple vow and might marry after resigning their stall. They too performed their choir offices and enjoyed a recognised status in the Church. The life of a mediaeval abbess was one of varied activities and responsibilities: in some cases her power was such that the diocesan bishop could perform no function within her jurisdiction save with her consent. In short, up to the time of the Reformation, the Church, while it assumed without discussion that women could not be priests, made full use of their consecrated service. It accorded to them a position of honour and dignity, and provided the only career open to them; apart from that of matrimony.

With the dissolution of the nunneries women lost their official place in the Church, and the opportunities for service which remained arose chiefly from their duties as Christian wives and mothers. In the feudal era the lady, or loaf-giver, was concerned with the religious, moral and physical well-being not only of her own children but of her lord's tenants.

The tradition that women of the upper classes should care for the souls and bodies of their poorer neighbours continued after the feudal tie had loosened, and blossomed into new life in the Victorian age. Family prayers were conducted daily by the master or mistress of the house. The latter had a Bible class for the younger maids, which paved the way for their communion.

Cecilia M. Ady, *The Role of Women in the Church* (London: The Central Council for Women's Church Work, 1948), pp. 13–14

In time, the very structures of the ordered society described by Cecilia Ady would break down. Women invested much in such change. They had, after all, been campaigning for it for over a century.

If we are to facilitate marriage, which must form, at any rate, the main solution of the problems of the near future, if we are to prevent, or even lessen, the degradation of women, if we are to extinguish this pit of destruction in our midst, into which so many a fair and promising young life disappears, and which perpetually threatens the moral and physical welfare of our own sons, if we are to stay the seeds of decay in our own nation, we must be content to revolutionize much in the order of our own life.

Ellice Hopkins, *The Power of Womanhood; or, Mothers and Sons* (London: Wells Gardner, Darton & Co., 1899), p. 153

I believe the day is near when women will no longer be the plaything of men's vices, or the storehouse for man's lust; they

will rise to the divine attitude, and fill the moral agency designed
for them by the great Creator. Then, and not until then, will the
scales fall from their eyes, and the shackles from their limbs, and
one with God they will work for the purification of all nations and
the honour and glory of their homes, their children and their sex.
The gladness, the heartaches and the tears of the home belong
equally to the husband and wife; the vote the husband casts is for
the wife, so is the whiskey he drinks, the tobacco he chews, the
pipe he smokes, and the money he squanders at gambling and
with other women.

Sister Emily, *Was Eve Guilty?*

(London: Messrs Hill, Cook & Lane, n.d.), pp. 41–2

*A twofold agenda for change is 'told out' by accounts such as
these. Their primary emphasis is on what would nowadays be
called the 'empowerment of women'. Miss Buss and Miss Beale
inculcated a sense of power by stamping on any 'deplorable show
of weakness' in their charges. In this passage, and in the two
that follow, attention should be paid to the vigorous, active
language which the writers use, and especially to the power of
their verbs.*

Another subject on which Frances Mary and Dorothea were in
perfect agreement was the schoolgirl propensity to faint: to both
Heads fainting was a deplorable show of weakness, and they dealt
with it accordingly. They knew very well that if one girl fainted at
Prayers others would follow suit; they realised that a girl might
faint, not from ill-health but from a desire to make herself the
centre of attention. Many are the stories of sharp reprimands
delivered to those unfortunate girls who had had the temerity to
disobey. A North Londoner recalled how her neighbour at
Prayers had fainted one day and how as soon as the girl recovered
sufficiently she removed her unobtrusively from the Hall. Afterwards Miss Buss sent for the helper, scolded her and told her how
she should have behaved. 'Once', she said, 'I was in church with a
pewful of girls. I noticed that one of them looked like fainting. I

leant across to her, shook my fist at her and said: "You dare faint."
And she didn't.'

Josephine Kamm, *How Different from Us:*
A Biography of Miss Buss and Miss Beale
(London: The Bodley Head, 1958) pp. 226–7

*Florence Nightingale got her way by a comparable show of
strength.*

When Florence Nightingale could not get drugs or bandages or
dressings for her sick and wounded soldiers, because the right
kind of order had not come from the right kind of army official,
she called the sentry in and told him to force open the doors
with his bayonet. That is the sort of thing that I think of. To go
to the Bible, there was David's act when his friends went
through the hosts of the Philistines to bring him a drink of
water, and 'when he saw it, he said, "Shall I drink of the blood
of these men who went in jeopardy of their lives for my sake?"
Therefore he did not drink it, but he poured it out before the
Lord.'

A. Maude Royden, *Here and Hereafter*
(London: Putnam, 1933), p. 217

*Leonora Eyles would have approved. She would 'hammer' certain
truths home.*

A certain type of woman, too, is still at the mercy of her
'femininity'. She can do a job perfectly well, but is quite ready to
accept masculine help in doing it, which rather discredits the
whole of women's work. Such women, however, are not serious
workers, they are working either because they need the money,
because life at their parents' home bores them, or simply to mark
time until they can find a man to marry them. Education, less
sheep-like than it is at present, will eradicate this type of girl by
teaching her responsibility and independence, and hammer into

her head the fundamental idea that chivalry is not the exclusive
prerogative of the male.

Leonora Eyles, *Careers for Women*
(London: Elkin Mathews & Marrot, 1930), p. 28

*But another note is also struck in these passages. An agenda for
change is one which affects men as well as women. For this reason,
tempting voices would continue to call women to order in the name
of subservience, but a new and very distinctive male voice would
also throw down a challenge to the churches. The ensnaring voice
of the Abbé Huvelin is a fascinating one. He contrasts the
'language of the heart' with the language 'of the world'.*

We need not be modern in our language or in our mode of life in
order to love our own times. You criticise in certain young women
and girls ideas, ways of looking at things, behaviour which is too
modern, and men are the first to criticise this conduct. Certainly
they will not look among these fast women for a companion on
life's long journey, for that there must be more solid goodness
than is found in a woman of the world. A really worldly woman is
a clever woman with a narrow mind, full of little falsities. Yes, a
woman of the world is very clever at making herself agreeable, at
speaking the sort of language which suits each person; she knows
how to lead astray, but she does not know how to love. By
thinking constantly of herself, making herself the one and only
object of her thoughts, her heart hardens, she becomes indifferent
to the sufferings of others, she cannot understand the language of
the heart. She meets the best and most devoted people, only to
break their hearts. One may laugh at a stupid person, perhaps,
but if she is good at heart we shall not laugh for long, we shall
forgive her foolishness because of her good qualities.

Abbé Huvelin, *Addresses to Women*
(London: Burns & Oates, 1936), p. 131

*How heartening, in contrast, to find the writings of Canon Raven.
He wrote a book entitled* Women and Holy Orders *in 1928.*

But along has come a change even more fraught with possibilities, a change which is altering the whole basis of human life and silently reforming for good or evil each one of us. This change has been achieved by the higher education of women and is symbolized by their admission to equal citizenship: and whether as triumph or as tragedy, it is by far the most critical element in the whole of the present situation. For in overthrowing the traditional relationship of the sexes it affects something as old as Eden, and far more fundamental than any matter of nationality, or class, or material possessions or philosophies or creeds. 'He for God only, she for God in him'; he the breadwinner, she the housewife; he the leader, she his subordinate; he to endow, she to obey; however we phrase it, here is an assumption as old as the cave-dweller or the anthropoid ape, an assumption which has controlled the whole social existence of mankind. And we in the twentieth century are witnessing the abandonment of that assumption, and are almost oblivious of the immense and incalculable consequences that will inevitably follow.

Queer is it not? that we should fill the presses with news about aeroplanes and wireless, housing and armaments, racial contacts and the League of Nations: and yet give hardly a thought to an issue beside which such topics seem almost ephemeral trifles. We read with admiration of the success of a woman swimmer or a woman architect, and are mildly interested in the Flapper Vote, and send our daughters away to school and college and out into the professions. But of the revolution in which we and they are assisting we seem almost unconscious. It is perhaps a proof of the magnitude of the event that its coming should pass unnoticed. Perhaps the other great and radical changes came similarly unannounced – when man learned to domesticate the animals, when he became an agriculturist, when he gave up the nomadic for the settled habitation, when he built the first city or designed the first boat, when Babylon, Egypt, Rome fell into decay. We like to think that history is the record of great men and dramatic events; and that is in its measure true. But there are moments slower and less public of which the world has hardly been aware and whose authors have left no memorial except a changed world; movements involving a vast unnamed mass of ordinary men and

women through whose half-conscious agency life was transformed.

It is no part of our present purpose to describe the emancipation of woman or to predict its influence. To do so would need
historical research and prophetic insight – and treatment on the
grand scale. Our concern is merely to question the change that is
taking place; to urge that it is by far the most critical issue of the
day; and then to consider what should be the attitude of the
Church towards one consequence of it, the claim for the admission of women to Holy Orders.

Charles E. Raven, *Women and Holy Orders: A Plea to the Church
of England* (London: Hodder & Stoughton Ltd, 1928), pp. 12–16

For me, and I think for the immense majority of us, nothing is
more obviously Christian than the change from the old regime to
the new. We are sure that the Spirit of God is manifest in the
development of girls' schools, the admission of women to
Universities, the opening of the professions to them. We believe
that on the whole the Women's Movement is the noblest and most
Christian achievement of the past century. 'By their fruits ye shall
know them': we know how fine are the fruits of the new
womanhood; we are thankful for what they are giving and will
give to the world; and to deny the worth of their higher education
and equal citizenship would be for us the sin against the Holy
Ghost: it would be to ascribe to Beelzebub what is evidently of
God.

Charles E. Raven, *Women and Holy Orders: A Plea to the Church
of England* (London: Hodder & Stoughton Ltd, 1928), pp. 35–6

If woman's freedom is of God, and if she needs His help to use it
aright, the Church cannot be blind to its obligation.

If this thing is of God, then surely the Church as the expression
and instrument of God's Spirit cannot refuse to welcome and use
it. Women have won their entrance into all the learned professions: they have risen to eminence in art and architecture,
medicine and education; they are establishing themselves in the

law-courts and the House of Commons; in every sphere of life except the fighting services their help is welcomed. For they have proved that they are qualified and that the new and highly educated type of womanhood has a great contribution to make to the welfare of the world. Only in the Church is the old order still dominant: only in the Church is there no free scope for the exercise of their talents by women: only in the Church is it assumed that women are by the fact of sex inferior to men and incapable of service except under conditions of strict subservience.

Charles E. Raven, *Women and Holy Orders: A Plea to the Church of England* (London: Hodder & Stoughton Ltd, 1928), pp. 41–2

This chapter has examined how women brought to each other the authority of a history of their own; the possibility of powerful role models through the examples provided by this history; and hence a sense of what they could be and become. The importance of these insights for both men and women was underlined as they gained allies for what would become known as 'The Cause', namely women's suffrage. When women could vote, their sense of identity and personal empowerment would bear fruit.

CHAPTER 8

~~

THIS RELEASE OF
WOMEN'S POWER

'I will sing of loyalty and of justice; to you, O Lord, I will sing'
(Psalm 101.1)

On November 21, 1865, a serious discussion on woman's right to participate in public affairs was held by the Kensington Society, which met at the house of a Mrs Manning to debate topics of the day as they related to women. Emily Davies was present and so were Jessie Boucherett, Elizabeth Garrett, Sophia Jex-Blake, Frances Mary Buss, Dorothea Beale and Mary Wolstenholme. Barbara Bodichon read a paper on the suffrage which was received with such enthusiasm that she wanted there and then to found a women's suffrage committee. The timing seemed right to her, for earlier in the year Emily Davies with Bessie Rayner Parkes and Isa Craig had driven about Westminster in a hired carriage covered with placards asking for votes for John Stuart Mill, who had been invited by the citizens of Westminster to stand for Parliament. Mill, who was a keen supporter of women's suffrage, had accepted only on condition that he would not be required to canvass or take any interest in local affairs and, rather surprisingly, his conditions had been accepted.

Josephine Kamm, *Rapiers and Battleaxes* (London:
George Allen & Unwin Ltd, 1966), p. 127

The names of the great and the good who first campaigned for the vote for women are recorded here by their biographer Josephine

Joan of Arc's Entry into Orleans

Kamm. These are the women who, in the words of Psalm 101, would link loyalty and justice as part of their Christian commitment. Secular feminist historians are sometimes embarrassed by the Christian heritage from which the suffrage movement emerged. They are reluctant to comment on it or to make connections between the sense of empowerment which these women clearly experienced and their reading of the gospel. And equally, religious historians are embarrassed by the involvement of Christian women in a political campaigning movement. After all, these were extremists. Theirs was a minority cause. It can easily be forgotten. That is why it is so important to reclaim the honourable Christian roots of the suffrage movement; to examine its use of Christian language and metaphors; and to explore what it discovered in the light of the Christian gospel.

Those who question the value and importance of this task beg all sorts of questions. Why should the religious inspiration of the suffragettes be written out of the history books? Why should the Christian churches find it so hard to honour them? At the time there were a plethora of women's groups and organizations which sought inspiration in the texts of the scriptures. The strong voices of individual women who had heard a call to personal identity are listed here. What is remarkable is that they also wanted to work corporately. Their sense of self did not lead them into autonomy; rather, it helped them to come together to federate and campaign. For this reason it is worth remembering how strong the ties between their inspiration and actions really were. The evidence is clear. Women grouped together and formed societies such as the following: the Catholic Women's Suffrage Society; the Church League for Women's Suffrage; the Free Church League for Women Suffrage; the Friends' League for Women's Suffrage; the Scottish Churches' League for Woman Suffrage.

An indication of how these groups were set up and organized can be gained by examining the story of the Scottish League. The Women's Who's Who takes up the tale:

This League was formed at a public meeting, held in the Goold Hall, Edinburgh, on 11th March, 1912, to express the recognition by the churches of the spiritual equality of the sexes, and the justice of the principle of their political equality.

A devotional service was held on Sunday afternoon, 26th May, in the Queen's Hall, Edinburgh, when the Rev. I. Maclean Watt, B.D., Minister of St. Stephen's Parish Church, gave an admirable and convincing address, which has since been printed by the League, and is being widely circulated.

During the summer, literature regarding the League was sent to the secretaries of guilds and other societies connected with the principal churches throughout Scotland, as a result of which members joined from many different towns and villages. A resolution – 'That this League protests against the non-inclusion of women in the Franchise Reform Bill now before Parliament' – was sent to each member of the Cabinet and to each Scottish M.P. A meeting to consider the religious aspect of the women's movement is to be held on 12th March next, in Edinburgh, when prominent ministers of various denominations are expected to take part.

CONSTITUTION

OBJECT – To unite on a non-party basis members or adherents of any of the Scottish Churches who are in favour of Woman Suffrage, in order to secure for women the Parliamentary Vote on the same conditions as men.

METHODS – The work shall be carried on by religious and educational methods, and shall include the distribution of literature and the holding of meetings for devotion and conference.

MEMBERSHIP – All men and women who are members or adherents of any of the Scottish Churches, and who approve of the League, may become Members on payment of an annual subscription of not less than one shilling.

A. J. R., *The Suffrage Annual and Women's Who's Who*
(London: Stanley Paul & Co., 1913), pp. 105–6

This blend of the practical and the devotional characterizes the work of this and comparable leagues. They provided a forum where women and men could work together for change; they also brought together 'adherents of any of the Scottish Churches', and so provide a nice example of early ecumenism. The membership lists are impressive and provide evidence of the existence of the kind of men of whom Almon Hensley wrote. She dedicated her book to her husband:

THIS BOOK IS DEDICATED TO MY HUSBAND
WHOSE BELIEF IN THE
FEMINIST MOVEMENT
AND WHOSE UNFAILING TRUST AND
SYMPATHY HAVE HELPED TO MAKE
THE WRITING OF IT POSSIBLE.

In the text she notes that

The really strong-minded and far-seeing man is not opposed to woman suffrage. The men who, demanding the full measure of their rights for themselves, are denying the most obvious justice to women, are either of the brutal, physically-dominating type of man who really desires a cowed mistress, not a help-meet for a wife – or the little man who is terrified lest he lose the only real power he possesses, the authority that to-day is attached to his sex.

Almon Hensley, *Love and the Woman of Tomorrow*
(London: Drane's, 1913), p. 63

The hope and the expectation were bright. The contribution of women to public life would transform the world. Frances Willard's exultant text highlights the importance of a sense of identity for women. This is precisely what having the vote would make plain and clear.

Miss Willard's faith in the power of womanhood was unbounded and every woman who listens to the brave sweet ideals which Frances Willard has left as a priceless legacy to her sex must win new faith and hope, and find her own ideals immeasurably uplifted. Speaking of the new ideal of womanhood, she has said: 'The world is slowly making the immense discovery that not what woman *does*, but what she *is*, makes home a possible creation. It is the Lord's ark, and does not need steadying; it will survive the wreck of systems and the crash of theories, for the home is but the efflorescence of woman's nature under the nurture of Christ's gospel. She came into the college and elevated it, into literature and hallowed it, into the business world and ennobled it. She will come into government and purify it, into politics and cleanse its Stygian pool, for woman will make homelike every place she enters, and she will enter every place on this round earth.'

W. J. Wintle and Florence Witts, *Florence Nightingale and Frances E. Willard: The Story of Their Lives* (London: Sunday School Union, n.d.), pp. 95–6

One of the very first women Members of Parliament conveys something of the spiritual sense which motivated the desire for change.

A new edifice is to be built by those of the present age. Women, it is generally accepted, are more constructive than destructive; and though men and women can only achieve completely as they work together, many are persuaded that, for some generations to come, women will be the chief architects of humanity. Disability after disability, hitherto hindering woman's power, is at this moment being swept away from her path with almost alarming rapidity. Profession after profession is being opened to her. Bill after Bill is being brought into the House of Commons today, doing away with existing inequalities and throwing open to women as well as men almost every path of life. It is practically certain that in the very near future every woman in the land will have the right to vote, to sit either in the House of Lords or House of Commons, and to enter all paths of professional and industrial life. Not only in one strata of society, but in all, this release of women's power is being felt, and very soon it will be felt yet more powerfully than now.

Edith Picton-Turberville, *Christ and Woman's Power*
(London: Morgan & Scott Ltd, 1919), pp. 114–15

Edith Picton-Turberville is quite unselfconscious about using 'Christ's power' in her title and then writing about women's power in her text. She was clear that the real issue was about power. Hence the interest of her judgement on the key players in the suffragette and suffragist movements.

I do not think the work of any human being who, when in the zenith of their activities were scoffed at, persecuted and reviled by those in authority as well as of the general public has been so swiftly and publicly recognised as was the work of Mrs. Pankhurst. When as a Member of Parliament I was at the unveiling of her statue in Palace Gardens by the ex-Prime Minister, Mr. Baldwin delivered a great oration in praise of the woman who less than twenty years before had been almost hounded to her death by the then Prime Minister of England.

I was never a follower of Mrs. Pankhurst's and had the courage to hold up my hand against her resolution at a vast Albert Hall meeting which was almost insane with enthusiasm. This action of mine was met with amused and tolerant laughter. With regard to the suffrage question Mrs. Fawcett was my leader and I was privileged to be present when a medallion in memory of her was unveiled in Westminster Abbey. If Mrs. Pankhurst was a crusader Mrs. Fawcett was a statesman, and who can say which was the most effective in securing the final victory and winning for the nation a really democratic franchise? On one point I do feel confident. I would never have had the interesting and absorbing experience of being a Member of Parliament had it not been for the work of these two gallant women.

Edith Picton-Turberville, *Life is Good*
(London: Frederick Muller Ltd, 1939), pp. 111–12

The word 'crusader' is used often in suffragette literature. Other religious symbolism and imagery can be detected in accounts such as this:

On April 16th a procession was held, and marched from the Marble Arch to the Aldwich Theatre to celebrate the release of Mrs. Pethick-Lawrence. The procession was led, on a day of bright spring sunshine, by Miss Elsie Howey, the daughter of the Rector of Finningley, in Nottinghamshire: wearing armour and carrying a banner of the Union colours, she rode astride a heavy but splendid white horse. Although the connection of the Maid with the ladies who attempted to march to the English House of Commons – and it was doing this on February 24th that Mrs. Lawrence had been arrested – was not obvious, the explanation of the prominence of the French patriot on this occasion was that two days later Joan of Arc was to be beatified at St. Peter's, Rome. The procession was a long one with an immense display of Union colours; included in it was a carriage, draped in the Stars and Stripes, which carried the American delegates to the International Suffrage Society which was meeting in London at this time.

Roger Fulford, *Votes for Women*
(London: Readers' Union/Faber & Faber, 1958), pp. 172–3

Joan of Arc was taken up by many of the campaigners as a champion of the cause, especially by those who chose to ride 'astride'.

'Did no one tell you to wear the dress of a man?'

'No one told me,' she said. 'If it is wrong, it is I who have done it.'

Then they said, 'Do you not think it wrong to dress yourself like a man?'

'In the name of God, why do you occupy yourselves with such trifles? It is a matter of no moment to you how I dress. When I live among men it is more decent that I dress like a man.'

They said, 'Would you take a women's dress if we allowed you to hear mass?'

She had a great desire to hear mass. She hesitated and said, 'I would take a woman's dress, but I beseech you to let me hear it as I am. This does not offend God.'

There is a hideous terror behind this trifling question of the dress of Joan of Arc, for a woman to dress as a man was heresy, and they wanted to prove that she was a heretic and a witch.

A. Maude Royden, *Blessed Joan of Arc*
(London: Sidgwick & Jackson Ltd, 1923), pp. 86–7

But the cause would also have its martyrs; the heresy charge was levelled again and again. Religious language and imagery are again called into service in this account, which describes the funeral procession for Emily Wilding Davison. An Oxford graduate in English, she threw herself under the King's horse at the Derby in 1913.

On Saturday, June 14th, her body was borne in triumph from Victoria to King's Cross with a pageantry which recalled the obsequies of princes. Thousands of women took part in the cavalcade – marching in groups dressed in black, purple or white – those wearing black carried purple irises; those in purple, red peonies and those in white, laurels. At the head of the procession were the usual mounted outriders immediately followed by a standard-bearer, with a banner, on which was embroidered 'Thoughts have gone forth whose power can sleep no more. Victory. Victory.' Then followed hunger strikers, the clergy, standard-bearer with a banner: 'Greater love hath no man than this that a man lay down his life for his friends', personal friends, the body, relations, a standard-bearer and banner: '*Dulce et decorum est pro patria mori*', hunger strikers, Mrs. Pankhurst's carriage, a standard-bearer and banner: 'He that loseth his life shall find it.' Members of the Union, women doctors and women graduates and a double band closed the great procession. A halt was made at St. George's Church, Bloomsbury, where the Reverend C. E. Baumgarten conducted a short service. The Great Northern Railway then bore the coffin northwards for burial in the grave of the Davison family in Morpeth.

Roger Fulford, *Votes for Women*
(London: Readers' Union/Faber & Faber, 1958), p. 251

The following year, thousands would go to their graves. With the advent of the First World War nothing would ever be the same again. Ray Strachey describes what this would mean for the cause.

Another change, even more vital to the Women's Movement than the approval of public opinion, was brought about by the war years, and that was a change in the outlook of women themselves. For the first time hundreds of thousands of them had experienced the joys of achievement; they had been of consequence and had done things they felt to be important; they had been encouraged to show enterprise and ambition, and they had been more or less adequately paid. The false and temporary prosperity of the war period had given women a taste of the power of money; the factory women had been better fed, in spite of the food shortage, than in the days when they did 'women's work' in their homes. The married women had had the spending of the separation allowances, and their children were better dressed and in better health than had ever been the case before. They saw what the world was like for men; and neither Act of Parliament nor season of reaction, nor any other thing could thereafter take that knowledge from them.

Ray Strachey, *The Cause*
(London: G. Bell & Sons Ltd, 1928), p. 348

This is the language of knowledge and empowerment, a revisiting of the Garden of Eden, with women now cast in the victors' role. The irony, of course, is that a betrayal would be enacted. People have short memories; they would soon forget about the religious conviction which women brought to the cause. They would forget that its language and banners and hymns and artefacts used Christian imagery. They would, however, discover that human nature remained as unreformed as ever, even after the vote was granted to women. In the words of the North American journalist Beatrice Fairfax, they would 'take the privilege for granted'.

How the young wage earners take the privilege of a job for granted! Thrown with many of them in my business of reporting, I've often been amazed to realise their ignorance of the fact that jobs for women are a modern invention. And they are actually unfamiliar with the names of those pioneer women who gave their time, strength, fortune, even life itself to women's cause. Occasionally some pretty girl with a job that enables her to live well, dress well, enjoy cultural advantages, if she has a taste for them, or make bi-weekly pilgrimages to a beauty parlour and a cocktail lounge, if that's her preference, will ask me, 'Who were these women? – Elizabeth Cady Stanton, Susan B. Anthony, Lucy Stone – some sort of reformers, weren't they, who wore funny clothing?'

'Reformers, indeed,' I answer; hardly trusting myself at the moment to say anything more.

In the early Beatrice Fairfax days, we young members of the Hen Coop were better informed about these matters than girls are today. We knew how hard jobs were to get and hold. As to the legal disabilities of married women, even though we might never have heard any old wives' tales, we had hundreds of letters pouring into our department which fully enlightened us.

We girls were all confirmed suffragists; but so far as writing about the subject went, our hands were largely tied. The big shots on the paper were not interested in woman suffrage in the beginning of the 1900's. Mr. Brisbane often said that the majority of women didn't want to vote. Mr. Charles Edward Russell, who later became an ardent feminist, was lukewarm on the subject: Mr. Ferralley, the delightful Irishman, always countered with something to the effect that if women were given more power than nature gave them, men would soon be begging for suffrage or have to retire to desert islands.

We of the Hen Coop religiously followed up the small parlour meetings that women used to hold in those days; and took enormous pains with the reports that we wrote of them. These, if they weren't discarded altogether, were always boiled down to a sentence.

It was pure chance that pointed out to us a crafty and guileful route to use in order to land such pieces in the paper. Some sort of altercation actually did occur to one of those parlour meetings. It didn't amount to anything, scarcely seemed worth mentioning; but to the masculine hierarchy it seemed to be amusing and they published it in full. Next time we got suffrage assignments to cover, we were told to watch out for 'fights'. Not only did we watch for them, but we actually created them, aided and abetted by those splendid pioneer suffragists who had been working for the amendment for nearly fifty years.

Beatrice Fairfax, *Ladies, Now and Then*
(London: John Gifford Ltd, 1944), pp. 156–7

A gloss on this text is provided by Edith Picton-Turberville.

It is for such reasons as this that from a Christian point of view unions of industrial women should be welcomed. If those who believe in the power of Christ, in faith and prayer, will stand beside them and 'not watch the procession, but walk in it,' such unions can become one of the most potent forces for Christianity in the twentieth century. The nations have just emerged from one of the most terrible catastrophes the world has ever seen; the effects of it are with us now, and maybe there are other catastrophes to follow. Ruskin points out that in every one of Shakespeare's plays catastrophe is brought about by the folly or fault of a man; the redemption, if there be any, is by the virtue and wisdom of a woman – and failing that, there is none!

Ruskin was a dogmatic teacher and not always right, but here he states a fact, whether Shakespeare had any deep meaning in it or not. Such things are easily said, and woman with her powers released has yet to prove herself; it is undoubtedly true that people of all classes are in these days looking to woman hopefully, almost pathetically, to redeem some of the evils of today. So great a task lies before her, that only by the faith and prayer of all Christian people can she hope to fulfil it. Recognizing what women are now being called to achieve, the demand that is being made upon their newly released powers, can anyone fail to see in the struggles of the Victorian pioneers the movement of the Holy Spirit preparing them for the task that lies before us today? Those who by lack of sympathy hindered woman's progress in days gone by, little thought that they were fighting against the advent of a power that at a critical time in the history of the world would seek to bring about a new order in harmony with the teaching of Christ. From the history of what women have achieved we may rest assured that women will use their power to build a new world, not for heroes to live in – men do not ask for that, but for something far simpler – a world fit for human beings who have an incurable desire, in spite of all that is said to the contrary, to link their lives with God and give all their children a chance to have happy thoughts of Him. Men and women can help or hinder by giving or withholding their sympathies, thoughts and prayers.

Edith Picton-Turberville, *Christ and Woman's Power*
(London: Morgan & Scott Ltd, 1919), pp. 135–6

In the event, human beings did not prove to be driven by an 'incurable desire to link their lives with God'. The spiritual message of Christabel Pankhurst is matched to the events of the day.

Various reasons forbid us to expect that, when other means are failing to save the world-situation, the votes of women will succeed.

Some of us hoped more from woman suffrage than is ever going to be accomplished. My own large anticipations were based partly upon ignorance (which the late war dispelled) of the magnitude of the task which we women reformers so confidently wished to undertake when the vote should be ours. Even had one suspected, in the days of the struggle for the vote, how vastly is the task beyond human power, whether of women or men, one would still have been without a better hope because of the ignorance of or indifference to Bible prophecy, from which, grievous to say, some politicians have not, even now, freed themselves.

Now for the reasons why women, like men, will be unable to mend the world by their votes, and the same is true even though women-voters be in the majority! To begin with, the vote itself is going down in value like Russian roubles or German marks. Yes, the political currency of the franchise is seriously debased. The decay of democracy, treated in the last chapter, accounts for this. We never took it into our calculations in the pre-suffrage, pre-war days. The solidarity and permanency of representative government we took for granted, never doubting that constitutional democracy would be adhered to in the letter and in the spirit. Upon that depended, of course, all the worth the vote could possibly have.

Arguing thus from false premises, we believed the vote would give to women a power, a practical influence upon events and conditions that it is not giving to them.

The rifle of a black-shirted Fascist, the industrial weapon of the striker, these are more potent in national affairs than the vote of a woman, and the balance is turning more against the vote as the days pass.

The receding tide of democracy cannot but leave the woman-voter high and dry.

Christabel Pankhurst, Pressing Problems of the Closing Age
(London: Morgan & Scott Ltd, 1924), pp. 38–9

In the event, the verdict of history has not proved so sombre. The vote was extended to women. Another war came and went. Democracy suffered and continues to suffer where the call to identity of nations, groups and individuals is not heard as a call from God. The call to all of us is a call to greater humanity. Only when the fullness of women's humanity had been endorsed by their gaining the vote could this be clear. In this sense the suffrage movement both began and ended in the gospel.

So who had taught this reading of the gospel to the young women who struggled for the Cause? That is what the next two chapters must examine.

CHAPTER 9

~

BREAKING THE BREAD OF
DIVINE KNOWLEDGE

'We will tell to the coming generation the glorious deeds of the Lord'
(Psalm 78.4)

We have met Dorothea Beale as a political campaigner; in this chapter she is identified with her other great cause, that of education.

I would fain dwell on the blessings of the increased moral influence of women, to a community which has learned to enter more fully into the Christian teaching of the equality of man and woman in the sight of God, – in opposition to that profane teaching of our great poet, which so marred the nobility of his character, and lowered the standard of right both for men and women,

'He for God only, she for God in him.'

It has been truly said that slavery degrades the slave owner even more than the slave, and all history teaches us, that those who treat women as incapable of thought, not as spiritual, responsible beings, are degraded – and we believe the change in opinion has had a vast spiritual influence for which we thank God and take courage.

The chief leaders in this great movement have surely 'deserved well of the republic'. Miss Buss, Miss Shireff, Mrs Grey, and Miss Emily Davies survive to look upon a world changed more than at the beginning could have been conceived possible. All has

Hannah More

been done quietly, patiently, gradually. The old idea of a 'lady' being one who came to be ministered to, is gone. To render service is felt to be the highest privilege, and it is mainly this desire that has made women contend for the means of education and training. This passion for service, as Ruskin has taught, stimulates every faculty, glorifies and gives insight into Nature, and hallows all art. This, as our great musicians have shown, ennobles the emotional nature, and exalts its expression. It energises and sustains the will, and gives happiness and peace which are far from selfish, – and so, women of culture and refinement pass daily from the table of Dives to minister to Lazarus.

Dorothea Beale, 'Postscript to Mrs Fawcett's Paper' in
The Cheltenham Ladies' College Magazine, Spring 1894, pp. 29–30

Miss Beale attributes the quest for education to a desire to serve; she demonstrates how education 'glorifies and ennobles and exalts' as well as producing women of culture and refinement. With Frances Mary Buss, she would do more for girls' education than any other single pioneer since the time of Hannah More. Cheltenham Ladies' College was and remains her most abiding legacy, just as the North London Collegiate School is a memorial to Frances Mary Buss. For both Miss Buss and Miss Beale, education was a Christian project. The education which girls would receive in the schools they founded would be a greater agent for social change than either of them could ever have imagined. Those who opposed the formation of an educated women's voice were equally persuaded of their gospel call. Was education part of the Christian endeavour, or was it not?

The need had always been there, as this account of the upbringing of the Wesley daughters reminds us.

In the seven Miss Wesleys, with their brains, their good looks, their strivings, their unhappiness, their limited chances in life, the parson's daughter first takes on a shadowy human form in history. Hitherto the parson's wife, with her family, has been almost completely behind the scenes. Who has ever given a thought to Mrs Ken, Mrs Andrewes, Mrs Jeremy Taylor, Mrs Fuller, Mrs Burnet, Mrs Tillotson – if such ladies ever existed at all? What did the wives of the seven Bishops think when their husbands were sent to the Tower? Nobody knows and nobody cares. They were still as much in the background, or nearly as much, as in the days when a discreetly kept mistress was less of a stumbling block than an honest wife. Much in the lives of the Wesley daughters was typical of the family history of the parsonage in the centuries that followed, while families were still overflowing and women were still economically dependent. In the next two hundred years innumerable girls were buried in remote rectories, clever and refined like the Wesleys, touched with genius now and then like the Bronteus and Jane Austen, captivating, perhaps like Gainsborough's Parson's Daughter; picking up an astonishing amount of education, sometimes at home, waiting for such husbands as their meagre opportunities brought them, sewing shirts and knitting socks for the brothers who went to school and college, and receiving the letters which later, perhaps, were to enlighten the early pages of those brothers' biographies, seeing the life of their generation in a natural limitation, as it seemed through their brothers' eyes.

There is said to be an old recipe for cooking a cutlet between two other cutlets – whereby the one became especially succulent at the expense of the others – which may be taken as a sort of parable of many of these sisters' lives. That the result of the process was a considerable number of faded companions, crushed governesses, poverty-stricken gentlewomen, and matrimonial misfits is not to be denied, though mercifully in life the elements of happiness are common things, the compensations often hidden from worldly eyes and not to be reckoned in the figures of the economist and the sociologist. We are in a bad way if happiness, among the clergy of all classes, is to be estimated in purely material terms.

In the case of Mrs Wesley there were spiritual compensations when she was an old woman and a widow, cared for by her surviving children. Moore's description of her death recalls the passing of Christiana in the *Pilgrim's Progress*. Ten days before it happened her son John had arrived in London from one of his ministering journeys. 'He found her on the borders of eternity, free from all doubt and fear, and from every desire but (as soon as God should call) to depart and to be with Christ.'

With her intellect, her character, her power of expressing herself in words and her influence, through her sons, on religious history, it seems a little strange that Susannah Wesley has not cut more of a figure among the women who have been classed as great. Perhaps the reason for her remaining in the background was that it was there that her work was done. Hers was an indirect influence; she made no contribution of her own to philanthropy, science, or literature, like Elizabeth Fry or Florence Nightingale or Elizabeth Barrett Browning. For that reason, probably, she does not take a place among the great, for all the heroic elements in her.

Not much, it seems, has been written of her individually.

Kirk's *Mother of the Wesleys* appeared in 1876, before the horrible word 'debunking' had been invented, or the sport of taking the Victorians (and other serious people) down a peg or two had been discovered in an age of post-war disillusionment. It is interesting to muse on the treatment she might have received from a biographer of the school of Lytton Strachey. Her views on education, for instance would lend themselves admirably to such ironic malice as Strachey pours on Dr Arnold of Rugby. 'The stern and dignified headmaster was actually seen to dandle infants, and to caracole upon the hearthrug on all fours.' Perhaps the fact that she was not a Victorian saved her from being hung with Arnold and Florence Nightingale in that coldly lighted gallery.

Margaret H. Watt, *The History of the Parson's Wife*
(London: Faber & Faber Ltd, 1943), pp. 55–6

Few girl children enjoyed the opportunities of Sir Allen Apsley's daughter.

'When I was about seven years of age, I remember, I had at one time eight tutors in several qualities, language, music, dancing, writing, and needlework; but my genius was quite averse from all but my book, and that I was so eager of that my mother, thinking it prejudiced my health, would moderate me in it; yet this rather animated than kept me back, and every moment I could steal from my play I would employ in any book I could find, when my own were locked up from me.'

Sir Allen [Apsley, Lieutenant of the Tower of London], proud of his little girl's intelligence, had her taught Latin; and though her tutor, his Chaplain, was 'a pitiful dull fellow,' and though her brothers 'had a great deal of wit,' she got far ahead of them in the race for learning.

At music and dancing she confesses that she did not excel –

'. . . and for my needle, I absolutely hated it. Play among other children I despised, and when I was forced to entertain such as came to visit me, I tired them with more grave instructions than their mothers', and plucked all their babies [i.e., dolls] to pieces, and kept the children in such awe that they were glad when I entertained myself with elder company.'

Dorothy Margaret Stuart, *The Girl Through the Ages*
(London: George G. Harrap & Co. Ltd, 1933), p. 186

Most uneducated girls were like the children of Cheddar who first attracted Hannah More's intervention.

Hannah herself described her new project in a letter to Elizabeth Caxter: 'A friend of mine and myself, having with great concern discovered a very large village at many miles distance from me, containing incredible multitudes of poor, plunged in an excess of vice, poverty and ignorance beyond what one would suppose possible in a civilised and Christian country, have undertaken the task of seeing if we cannot become humble instruments of usefulness to these poor creatures, in the way of schools, and a little sort of manufactory. The difficulties are great, and my hopes not sanguine; but He who does not "despise the day of small things" will, I trust, bless this project. I am going directly down to my little colony to see what can be done before winter sets in.'

In a long letter to Wilberforce from the George Hotel, Cheddar, in 1789, Hannah tells him how she went to the chief man of the village, who was very rich. 'He begged that I would not think of bringing my religion into the country; it was the worst thing in the world for the poor, for it made them lazy and useless.' The farmers had told her that they might have a resident curate but that they were afraid their tithes would be raised if they applied for one! The parochial clergy themselves were not attentive to their duties, and of one of them Hannah writes in the same letter that he 'is intoxicated about six times a week; and very frequently is prevented from preaching by two black eyes, honestly earned by fighting.'

The first school was established at Cheddar, where a thatched cottage was taken on a lease for seven years and adapted for use as a school. When Hannah inquired what other places were destitute of religious privileges, she found that six large parishes from six to ten miles apart had no resident curate; there was evidently abundant scope for her evangelistic and educational efforts.

James Silvester, *Hannah More: Christian Philanthropist*
(London: Thynne & Co. Ltd, 1934), pp. 66–7

Hannah More would develop this theme in her commentary on women's education of 1800.

It is a singular injustice which is often exercised towards women, first to give them a very defective education, and then to expect from them the most undeviating purity of conduct; to train them in such a manner as shall lay them open to the most dangerous faults, and then to censure them for not proving faultless. Is it not unreasonable and unjust, to express disappointment if our daughters should, in their subsequent lives, turn out precisely that very kind of character for which it would be evident to an unprejudiced bystander that the whole scope and tenor of their introduction had been systematically preparing them?

Hannah More, *Strictures on the Modern System of Female Education*,
vol. 1 (London: T. Cadell Jun. & W. Davies, 1801), p. 3

She saw the task of education as part of her Christian duty, much as the women who were quietly educating girls in the Quaker and Roman Catholic schools of the time would do. She recruited colleagues to help her with this work, women who would visit and comfort and pray with their charges.

For the first year, these excellent women had to struggle with every kind of opposition so that they were frequently tempted to give up their laborious employ. They well entitled themselves to Thirty pounds per annum salary, and some little presents. We established a Weekly School of thirty girls, to learn reading, sewing, knitting and spinning. The latter, though I tried three sorts, and went myself to almost every clothing-town in the county, did not answer – partly from the exactions of the manufacturer, and partly from its not suiting the genius of the place. They preferred knitting after the school hours on week-days. The mother or daughter visited the sick, chiefly with a view to their spiritual concerns; but we concealed the true motive at first; in order to procure them access to the houses and hearts of the people, they were furnished not only with medicine, but with a little money, which they administered with great prudence. They soon gained their confidence, read and prayed with them, and in all respects did just what a good clergyman does in other parishes.

Hannah More, *The Letters of Hannah More*
(London: The Bodley Head Ltd, 1925), pp. 168–9

Now this ministry of education and home visiting did not go unopposed. The force and vehemence of the Cheddar farmers' anger was directed against Hannah and her companions.

Some farmers in a parish adjoining, where there is also a school, have been to the fortune teller, to know if we are Methodists, and if our school is methodistical. The oracle returned an ambiguous answer, and desired to know what reason they had for suspecting it; the farmers replied, it was because we sung Watts's hymns. The sage returned for answer, this was no proof; had they no better reason? 'Yes,' they answered, 'for if the *hymns* were not methodistical, the *tunes* were.' The Pythian asked why they were so, the reply was, 'because they were not in Farmer Clap's book!'

I thought this fact ridiculous enough to amuse you. Yet these people are our judges; and there are not wanting those, who, though better taught, will listen to the representation of such accusers. In the midst of this clamour, poor Patty went down to the place two Sundays ago. The farmers called a vestry (to which she could not get admittance), to sign a paper to abolish the school. With great calmness she went on teaching the whole day. At night, about two hundred orderly people assembled as usual, but just as she was going to begin, two farmers came to the door, very tipsy, loudly vociferating that they would have no such methodistical doings, for that the sermon they had had in the morning was quite enough – their intoxication, however, did not give a very favourable evidence of its good effects. After they had spent their violence, Patty told them it would be a serious thing if they should die that night, after having attempted to disturb a people who were solely met for religious purposes. One of them said, 'How can you put such melancholy things in one's head, ma'am,' and ran out. She quietly went through the business to a most respectful audience, whose solemn attention rewarded her for what she had gone through. On Sunday, we are going, if I am able, again; whether the violence be found to be abated or inflamed, you shall know. I hope it may please God to endue us with a proper temper, and quiet perseverance, and that these trials may help to purify our motives. I am better myself, but we have much domestic sickness and sorrow. May all work together for good! God bless you and yours.

Hannah More, *The Letters of Hannah More*
(London: The Bodley Head Ltd, 1925), pp. 178–9

A modern commentator takes up the theme in this account of the history of headmistresses and their role as 'reluctant revolutionaries'.

The title chosen for this book may well have caused surprise, hilarity or plain disbelief, according to the cast of mind, among those who think that the word 'Revolutionaries' is the last that can or should be applied to head mistresses and who see them as people without marked revolutionary tendencies. Yet there are always radical processes occurring in society without violent upheavals or dramatic publicity which are nevertheless revolutions. It is in some of these that head mistresses, through past hundred years, have been leaders or catalysts.

The founders of the Association built up their schools and provided education for girls of the middle and upper class against a formidable wall of Victorian prejudice. It was prejudice about the role of women in society, about the dangerous effect that education might have on their willing acceptance of it, and about their essential inadequacy for any intellectual pursuit beyond the study of Mrs Beaton and the use of ready-reckoners for their accounts. A letter published in a women's magazine just two years before the meeting at Myra Lodge put the matter in a nutshell. 'We were asked', it ran, 'why we disapproved of public schools for girls and not for boys. Our reply was that girls were destined for private and domestic life and boys for public life and that their education should respectively correspond to the duties each has to perform in the future.'

Mary Price and Nonita Glenday, *Reluctant Revolutionaries:*
A Century of Headmistresses 1874–1974
(London: Pitman Publishing, 1974), p. 140

The point is well made. Education is a powerful force for change. For this reason, it is not morally neutral. Those who opposed the 'reluctant revolutionaries' were radically opposed to the change which education would bring about. They were aware that it would lead women to question their place in society. So what was education for domestic life? For life in the private world which women were supposed to inhabit? It is described and then dismissed by Dorothy Margaret Stuart in this lively account.

School-mistresses who were not themselves qualified to give instruction in more solid subjects salved their consciences and satisfied the parents of their pupils by teaching an enormous variety of more or less useless accomplishments.

Hannah Woolley, left an orphan at the age of fourteen, started a small school, and for two years 'was sole mistress thereof,' after which she became a governess in the family first of one 'Noble Lady' and then of another. She drew up a list of some twenty things in which she claimed especial skill: some of them, such as 'healing any wounds not desperately dangerous' and 'making Salves, Oyntments, Waters, Cordials,' are decidedly practical, but others, the vast majority, sound almost exasperatingly futile. Among the twenty were:

Works wrought with a needle, all Transparent Works, Shell-work, Mosswork,

also Cutting of Prints, also adorning Rooms
or Cabinets or Stands with them.
All kinds of Beugle-works upon wyers or otherwise.
Rocks made of Shell or in Sweets.
Feathers of Crewel for the corners of Beds.
Setting out of Banquets.
All manner of Cookery.
Writing and Arithmetic.
Washing black or white Sarsnets.
Making Sweet Powders for the Hair or to lay among Linnen.

Dorothy Margaret Stuart, The Girl Through the Ages
(London: George G. Harrap & Co. Ltd, 1933), p. 183

*The abuse of religion by using it to control girls is also condemned.
The contrary voices had to be countered.*

Those who have happily been educated within the last twenty or
thirty years can hardly realise what 'seminaries for young ladies'
were like in the early and middle nineteenth century. The two
years which Frances Cobbe spent at Brighton between 1836 and
1838, cost her parents with 'extras', the incredible sum of £1,000!
And the chief thing implanted in her young mind by the subjects
and method of tuition during that period was the resolve never to
trouble her head over learning anything else but 'to read novels
and amuse herself for the rest of her life.'

The system which, for the time, so effectually nipped in the
bud the girl's opening love of study was one which placed religion
and morals at the bottom of the scale of importance, and
accomplishments and deportment at the top. English, writing,
and arithmetic occupied a small space between.

No recreation whatever was allowed to these unhappy girls but
a dismal hour's walk, which they were permitted to enliven by
reciting French or German verbs to the governesses in charge;
but they were expected every day to don evening dress, of silk or
muslin, with gloves and kid slippers. And in this guise Miss
Cobbe remembered seeing on Saturday evenings – which were
devoted to the punishment of the accumulated sins of the week – a

row of big girls, some of them marriageable, sitting in disgrace in the corner, or with their faces to the wall. A notable point in the religious education of these young ladies was the provision of salt-fish on Ash Wednesday. This they were enjoined to partake of without the addition of a cut from the roast joint which came in – to be looked at – afterwards, because to fast was 'good for their souls and their *figures*.'

Jennie Chappell, *Women of Worth*
(London: S. W. Partridge & Co. Ltd, n.d.), pp. 99–100

The enlightened attitude of Hannah More stands in total contrast to this. Hers was a spiritual project. It would bear spiritual fruit.

I would have it understood that by these little comments, I do not mean that the child should be put to learn dry, and to her unintelligible, expositions; but that the exposition is to be colloquial. And here I must remark in general, that the teacher is sometimes unreasonably apt to relieve herself at the child's expense, by loading the *memory* of a little creature on occasions which far other facilities should be put in exercise. The child herself should be made to furnish a good part of this extemporaneous commentary by her answers; in which answers she will be much assisted by the judgement the teacher uses in her manner of questioning. And the youthful understanding, when its powers are properly set to work, will soon strengthen by exercise, so as to furnish reasonable, if not very correct answers.

Written forms of prayer are not only useful and proper, but indispensably necessary to begin with. But I will hazard the remark, that if children are thrown *exclusively* on the best forms, if they are made to commit them to memory, like a copy of verses, and to repeat them in a dry customary way, they will produce little effect on their minds. They will not understand what they repeat, if we do not early open to them the important *scheme* of prayer. Without such an elementary introduction to this duty, they will afterwards be either ignorant or enthusiasts or both.

Hannah More, *Strictures on the Modern System of Female Education*,
vol. 1 (London: T. Cadell Jun. & W. Davies, 1801), pp. 326–7

The educationalists received a sacred charge. They believed that they were touching sacred things when they taught God's word.

To Dorothea, to teach Scripture was an experience so deep and so wonderful that she longed to share it with every aspiring teacher. 'I should like most of you to look forward to Scripture teaching as a privilege to be desired', she told her staff. 'It is a sacred ministry, a sort of priesthood, this touching of sacred things, this breaking the bread of Divine knowledge for our children.'

Josephine Kamm, *How Different from Us: A Biography of Miss Buss and Miss Beale* (London: The Bodley Head, 1958), p. 244

Another account from a former pupil evokes the strength of this commitment.

It was for that fuller vision of holiness that Dorothea was striving to prepare herself and her 'children'. Her intense religious feelings could not fail to have an immense influence on the whole College. 'I shall never forget the impression I received as a quite young girl', wrote one of her pupils, 'when I heard her read the first chapter of St. John's Gospel. It was quite electric, one felt that this woman was reading the thing she considered the greatest in the world.' Even now, more than fifty years after Dorothea's death, those who heard her read St. John's Gospel still speak of the experience as unforgettable.

Josephine Kamm, *How Different from Us: A Biography of Miss Buss and Miss Beale* (London: The Bodley Head, 1958), p. 243

The women whose commitment to education was a work of evangelism quite consciously and deliberately brought the full force of the gospel to bear upon the developing consciousness of young women. They were opening the Scriptures and the message of the Scriptures to a rising generation. They were sowing seeds for change.

Leonora Eyles comments on the impact of higher education.

To anyone with an eye for social phenomena the conditions in this country since the beginning of the century are full of interest. We have seen, in this short space of time, an enormous increase of women's opportunities due partly to the Education Act of 1870, which widened their ideas by teaching them at least to read; due also to the pioneer work done by a few women in providing for the higher education of those who could not afford to pay for it. No longer now is every girl forced to live dependent on her parents or a husband, or become teacher, dressmaker, nurse, shop-assistant, or domestic worker. It was just before the war that the impact of the higher education of girls began to be felt in their determination to get outside the four walls of the home, but it was the way in which they stepped into the breaches left by the men on active service that proved their ability to do work they had never, even in their dreams, thought of doing before.

Leonora Eyles, *Careers for Women*
(London: Elkin Mathews & Marrot, 1930), pp. 15–16

The vision of the educators would be translated into the experience of those whom they taught. They had found an educated voice. All that was needed now was the fine tuning to make it an eloquent one. Girls' education was a paradigm for the Christian enterprise. The debate about what education was for (public life/private life) and whether or not women should receive it was in fact a debate about the extent to which the gospel was meant for everyone. Were women to 'tell out' the great mysteries of salvation in the public as well as the private domain, or were they not?

CHAPTER 10

~~

THE PARADISE OF WOMEN

'My soul magnifies the Lord' (Luke 1.47)

The project of education for women was a visionary one. The language used to describe girls' schools as a 'Paradise of Women' is eloquent. When Miss Willard was made the first President of the Evanston College for Ladies, her biographers became lyrical.

Meanwhile, a new and larger scene of action than any which she had previously occupied had opened before her. In Evanston, which Miss Willard designated as the paradise of women, it was decided to open a college for women entirely under women's control. Even in the advanced state of American college life, such an arrangement was an innovation. No woman had ever occupied the coveted position of College President, and therefore it was no slight token of the respect and esteem with which Evanston regarded the young teacher, when an invitation was given to Miss Willard to become the first President of the Evanston College for Ladies.

W. J. Wintle and Florence Witts, *Florence Nightingale
and Frances E. Willard: The Story of Their Lives*
(London: Sunday School Union, n.d.), p. 39

Those who emerged from the educational process would convert this lyricism into the hard currency of what Florence Nightingale would call 'the rules of business'. Her judgement on women sounds harsh when she associates inefficiency and sketchy work to them. But she early on had to confront the dilemma which many educated women would face.

Study and Work

Florence Nightingale has set an example of what a woman can do when she gives not only her mind, but *herself* to a thing. Having set the example, she has a right to advise. Here are some words of wisdom from her pen:

'I would say to all young ladies who are called to any particular vocation, qualify yourselves for it as a man does for his work. Don't think you can undertake it otherwise. No one should attempt to teach the Greek language until he is master of the language; and this can only become by hard study. If you are called to man's work, do not exact a woman's privileges – the privilege of inaccuracy, of weakness, ye muddleheads. Submit yourselves to the rules of business as men do, by which you alone can make God's business succeed; for He has never said that He will give His success and His blessing to inefficiency, to sketchy and unfinished work.'

> W. J. Wintle and Florence Witts, *Florence Nightingale*
> *and Frances E. Willard: The Story of Their Lives*
> (London: Sunday School Union, n.d.), p. 141

For some women this struggle was anything but 'paradisaical'. Mary Somerville was eleven years old when the disciplines of learning first began to open doors in her imagination and world-view.

One day, at the house of a friend, as she was looking in a magazine of a fashionable kind for a pattern of ladies' work, she came upon some letters oddly arranged – an algebraic problem. Asking the meaning, she heard the word Algebra for the first time. She thought about the word and took every opportunity that her great diffidence permitted to get further explanation. She was told of the need of arithmetic in the higher branches and mathematics. She thought some books in the home library might help her, and so she pored over some books of navigation; and though she made very little progress in what she wanted to know, she learned enough to open her mind to the value of solid studies and to interest her in them. Meanwhile, from some elementary books, probably her brother's, she began to teach herself Latin, and with no help of regular instruction learned enough to enable her to read Caesar's Commentaries, and to feel an interest in her reading.

Her habit of early rising was her great help, and enabled her to pursue her studies unmolested. She was very diligent in performing all that she was required to do in her daily domestic avocations, so that no fault could be found with her for neglecting anything required of her in the ordinary pursuits of life. Thus the lonely little student went on with her studies, until her progress was so considerable that when on a visit to her uncle, the Rev. Dr. Somerville, he found she had grounded herself both in Latin and Greek. He gave her books, and what was better, a word of encouragement, and she at length possessed a Euclid, and advanced into mathematics.

The word of encouragement must have been indeed precious from its rarity. She was not only laughed at but censured for the studies she applied herself to; 'going out of the female province' was then a common phrase of disapproval. Poor girl! it was to her, as it has been to multitudes in the old times of darkness and prejudice, a strange thing to find that the world recognised ignorance as the female province.

However, she persevered in all gentleness, yet with ceaseless energy. No one could say that she neglected any ladylike acquirements.

Clara Lucas Balfour, *Women Worth Emulating*
(London: Sunday School Union, 1907), pp. 8–9

This is education acquired at some cost. In old age Mary Somerville would nevertheless continue to thank God for the 'infinite mercy of an unimpaired intellect'.

Though she lived to be ninety-two, it can scarcely be said that she ever lost her youth, her intelligence remaining so clear, her spirits so fresh, her sympathies so active. Able to read without spectacles, to write to and converse with her friends; a slight deafness and a little tremor of the hands alone told that the vital energy was flagging, while her soul was light in the Lord. On principle, she said but little on her religious opinions, and never entered into controversy; but she was deeply and truly devout. One of her last written testimonies was: 'Deeply sensible of my own unworthiness, and profoundly grateful for the innumerable blessings I have received, I trust in the infinite mercy of my Almighty Creator. I have every reason to be thankful that my intellect is still unimpaired; and although my strength is weakness, my daughters support my tottering steps, and by incessant care and help make the infirmities of age so light to me that I am perfectly happy.'

Clara Lucas Balfour, *Women Worth Emulating*
(London: Sunday School Union, 1907), pp. 16–17

Some of the ways in which women acquired education were far from 'paradisaical', it has to be said. Mary Somerville kept her self-image intact; others, such as Caroline Herschel, the astronomer who discovered some eight comets, faired less well. From the start her mother wanted her to learn to knit, while her father had more lofty ambitions for her.

Caroline knew that her father grieved because her education was neglected, and as she knitted the eternal family stocking, she continued to attend the lessons he gave, paying particular heed to all his instructions. The mother was as determined as ever that Caroline should not be taught anything but the household routine. These contending influences, the misfortunes her family had suffered, all told upon the child; she fell into a low state of health, and was attacked by typhoid fever. She was so weak that, she says, 'for several weeks I was obliged to mount the stairs on all fours like an infant.'

Alice Corkran, *The Romance of Woman's Influence*
(London: Blackie & Son Ltd, n.d.), p. 150

She moved to her brother's house on the death of her parents. And there her training began.

Her training to an assistant astronomer began at once. It consisted of a most desultory form of education. At breakfast, every morning, the brother heard the sister's questions and answered them. She wrote the answers in a pocket-book. 'Your little head seems made of sand,' he said to her – 'everything can be inscribed upon it, and everything can as easily be effaced.' He was her only teacher. Her pocket-book contained a miscellaneous jumble of knowledge, elementary formulae, solutions of problems in trigonometry, rules for the use of tables of logarithms, for converting sidereal into solar time. With her pocket-book she carried about the multiplication table. 'She appears never to have spent a single hour in the systematic study of astronomy,' Miss Agnes M. Clarke says.

The brother and sister would begin the night work by making calculations of the double stars. She would always be by his side, always ready to answer his call, and it was not an automaton assistant that helped him. She was a living, breathing woman, vibrating with the excitement of those sweeping searchings of the heavens. And yet she thought she had little faculty to be an astronomer's assistant.

Alice Corkran, *The Romance of Woman's Influence*
(London: Blackie & Son Ltd, n.d.), pp. 170–1

Alice Corkran subtitles her book The Romance of Woman's Influence: ST. MONICA – VITTORIA COLONNA – MADAME GUYON – CAROLINE HERSCHEL – MARY UNWIN – DOROTHY WORDSWORTH AND OTHER MOTHERS, WIVES, SISTERS, AND FRIENDS WHO HAVE HELPED GREAT MEN. *Miss Balfour makes a more rigorous judgement.*

From this time, Miss Caroline Herschel became what, in her humility, she never desired to be – a celebrity. She rather shrank from any praise of herself, as if it was taken from her brother. He was to her as the sun, and she merely a shadow called up by his brightness. Surely, it was an absurd and exaggerated humility in her to say, 'I did nothing for my brother but what a well-trained puppy-dog would have done. I was a mere tool, which he had the trouble of sharpening.'

All the thoughtful people of her own time, and still more since the narrative of her life has been given to the world, will not take

THE PARADISE OF WOMEN

her own estimate of herself. She achieved individual, quite as much as relative greatness.

Space will not permit me to follow the career of Miss Herschel as an astronomer, except to remind my young readers that she did not allow herself to become less diligent as she grew more celebrated. A real love of science for its own sake, and not for any praise, still less for pecuniary advantage, possessed and ennobled her mind. She had the small salary of fifty pounds a year awarded her as assistant astronomer, and this was continued as a pension in her old age.

Her discovery of the first comet was followed by that of seven or eight others. After her brother's marriage, which took place late in his life to a very amiable lady, Miss Herschel removed to a small residence near him, and continued to sit up with him in his observatory, note down his observations and make necessary and difficult calculations for him. She was greatly delighted, with what may be called an almost maternal joy, when a son of that beloved brother was placed in her arms – that son who lived to nobly inherit his fathers' genius, and uphold and extend the fame of the honoured name of Herschel.

Of course, as celebrity came to her she was sought out by the wealthy and distinguished; but whether in the courtly sphere of royalty, or among the *elite* of fashionable and scientific circles, she always retained the unaffected simplicity of her manners, delighting all by her friendliness and entire freedom from assumption. She was a true gentlewoman in heart and manners, thinking always of others rather than herself.

Clara Lucas Balfour, *Women Worth Emulating*
(London: Sunday School Union, 1907), p. 51

It is hardly surprising that the next generation of scientists would become agnostic. Maude Royden rejoiced when another researcher, Madame Curie, discovered radium. She uses the phrase 'one of the saints of science' in her eulogy.

I glory in the knowledge that one of them – the discovery of radium – was the work of a woman, and a woman of such noble character, so self-regardless, so fine, so pure, as to make her one of the saints of science. Because such women exist I shall resent and denounce every attempt to dogmatize about 'woman's sphere' or to deny to women complete freedom to decide for themselves what they shall attempt and what is within their powers.

A. Maude Royden, *Women's Partnership in the New World*
(London: George Allen & Unwin Ltd, 1941), p. 26

Madame Curie's biographer, her daughter Eve, describes how this 'secular saint' dealt with the education of her own daughters.

She did not have her daughters baptized and gave them no sort of pious education. She felt herself incapable of teaching them dogmas in which she no longer believed: above all, she feared for them the distress she had known when she lost her faith. There was no anticlerical sectarianism in this. Absolutely tolerant, Marie was to affirm on many occasions to her children that if they wanted to give themselves a religion later on, she would leave them perfectly free.

Mme Curie was content that her daughters should know nothing of the uneasy childhood, drudging adolescence and poverty-stricken youth that had been hers. At the same time she did not wish for them to live in luxury. On several occasions Marie had had the opportunity of assuring a great fortune to Irene and Eve. She did not do so. When she became a widow she had to decide what to do with the gramme of radium that she and Pierre had prepared with their own hands, which was her private property. Against the advice of Dr Curie and of several members of the family council, she decided, sharing the views of him who was no more, to make to her laboratory a gift of this precious particle, which was worth more than a million gold francs.

In her mind, if it was inconvenient to be poor, it was superfluous and shocking to be very rich. The necessity for her daughters to earn their own living later on seemed healthy and natural to her.

Eve Curie, *Madame Curie* (London: Heinemann, 1938), p. 262

Eve Curie's was an extraordinarily popular book. Many of those which had previously celebrated the achievements of women were deliberately written as 'hagiographies'. They have titles like Women Who Have Worked and Won, Women of Worth, Women Who Ventured, Women Worth Emulating, Heroines of Mercy and Daily Life, Peerless Women, *and so on. Those which have survived frequently bear plates which indicate that they were awarded as Sunday-school prizes. They were written to edify; that is to say, to inspire and impress.*

But Eve Curie's account of her mother's life is part of a new narrative genre, written to explain rather than to edify. These books celebrate the achievement of women but rarely describe their faith context. The secularization of women's biography ran parallel with secularization in general. In the event the paradise dreamed up by early pioneers of education had to face up to the complexities of fallen human nature. The debate about what education is for would run and run.

An authoritative commentary on the dynamics of these two psychological and literary worlds was provided by the Christian women commentators. They would still use the language and metaphors of the tradition, but they would use them critically, in defence of new principles. Theirs was an educated voice. It judged both the pious and the professional worlds because it had been formed in both.

We hear much about 'the higher education of women' as a means of admission into several professions which have hitherto been regarded as accessible only by men, and society is, for the most part, coolly awaiting, with folded hands, the result of their efforts at competition in these professions. The several stages of opposition and ridicule have been surmounted. Women have been through the same college curriculum with men; have taken diplomas from schools of law, divinity, and medicine; and are now on trial before a jury which differs vastly from the ordinary array of 'twelve idiots' in that it represents, largely, the best thought of the day. It is plain to all that, if a woman essays to perform any work which is not, from its very nature, purely woman's work, she must, for the time being, ignore all considerations except those pertaining to the best achievement: hence she must accept judgement upon the work itself, the worker being practically ignored.

For us, the question is purely and exclusively womanly; and for me, coming to you as a teacher of what you 'ought to know,' the way is as straight and as plain as God can make it.

Mary J. Studley, *What Our Girls Ought to Know*
(New York: Holbrook & Co., 1881), pp. 223–4

There would be other texts which would make an equally telling judgement. As the thinking of educated women became more refined, as their voices became more finely tuned, how are we to react to what they said? After all, it is easy to endorse the work of the women hymn-writers and preachers, and that of the social and political campaigners. They fought for 'good' causes. The judgement of history has marched to their tune. But what about the educators? Did they somehow get it badly wrong? Did they launch women on a path which would lead inevitably to agnosticism?

We have seen that the sense of vision and purpose they brought to the task was indomitable. Education was understood to be part of the Christian enterprise and not separate from it. So how are we to read texts such as the following? As a joke, because some of them are quaint? As somehow maverick, because they advocated subjects like 'Recreative Education for Girls'? As redundant, because they were so evidently the voices of believing women, yet they were not properly heard? How are we to listen?

There were jokes, of course. These were women who kept their sense of humour, as we should keep ours.

A student teacher in a lesson on vegetable cookery upon being queried by a member of a perfectly docile and law-abiding class as to the nature of spinach, pronounced the word as 'SPINACK', and classified it on the blackboard as a root vegetable. A greengrocer's daughter present at the lesson, an authority on the subject of vegetables and a marked influence over the other members of the class, saw to it from that moment that neither she nor her companions paid the slightest attention to the subsequent theories or dictates of the teacher; contempt and lack of faith entered their ranks, and despite all the efforts of their young instructress neither good work nor courteous behaviour could be extracted from them.

Unless truth and accuracy, then, be the keynote of the subject-matter which the teacher imparts the advancement of housework along the lines of an educational craft can never be furthered. The Domestic teacher should make it her business to delve below the surface of superficially reasonable assumptions, many of which crumble upon investigation, and expound only that which she knows to be the fact; research should be her inflexible rule, and having constant recourse to text-books will ensure that facts are kept fresh in her memory – the best memory being far from infallible.

Elizabeth Atkinson, *The Teaching of Domestic Science*
(London: Methuen & Co. Ltd, 1931), p. 101

An honestly-made pudding will speak for itself, as likewise will one that has been the victim of a greedy child, who, thinking to gain some personal advantage, has helped herself too liberally to one or other of the ingredients, thus spoiling the whole. Similarly, a child who shirks the unattractive spadework of first ironing to dryness the double parts of a garment and hastens to the more fascinating job of ironing the lace and embroidery, will there and then be faced with the result of her negligence in the form of a disappointing effect in the work she has so much enjoyed.

Elizabeth Atkinson, *The Teaching of Domestic Science*
(London: Methuen & Co. Ltd, 1931), pp. 3–4

This is moral teaching of a high order. And it extends to the physical as well as the domestic order: to pudding-makers and to those who eat them.

It has long been said by prominent medical men that women themselves are responsible for a large share of their characteristic weaknesses, and the following extract from a note addressed to me by Dr. Willard Parker only echoes the prevailing sentiment of the profession. He says: 'Women kill themselves by their bad management in a mechanical way. They make themselves portable machines for effete matter. Their nerves cry out when fed by a dirty blood, and the cry is called neuralgia. What folly to give an anodyne for the neuralgia and let the cause of it remain!'

It is not strange that the gentlemen of the profession were limited to generalities in their charges against women for maltreatment of their bodies. They never wore the machinery with which the conventionally dressed women is deformed, and how could they attack its details or make any real progress toward reform! The real dress reform necessarily waited to be inaugurated by medical women, and its progress keeps pace with theirs toward popular acceptance. No woman who understands the beauty of the original design of the human body will ever seek to distort that body by subjecting it to the demands of a fashion which is totally regardless of natural laws; it therefore follows, as surely as day follows night, that the women who study medicine are the women who have most respect for their bodies and who have, therefore, the soundest and most serviceable bodies – bodies upon which they can count for any amount of intellectual or other work as surely as men can depend on their bodies.

Mary J. Studley, *What Our Girls Ought to Know*
(New York: Holbrook & Co., 1881), pp. 8–9

This is where recreative education comes into its own. Again there is something quaint about the text, but its focus was entirely on the well-being of the girls being educated. For this reason we should not dismiss it as maverick.

Recreative Education for Girls has scarcely received the attention in Literature that it demands. Much in this department has been done for Boys, for whom Science has been popularised, and active Games multiplied; but their young sisters have been allowed to waste too many of their home hours in frivolity and indolence, until they indeed come to regard the great world as a Nursery, or a Vanity Fair.

Intellectual pursuits awaken neither the envies nor the jealousies so apt to spring up in girlish bosoms. The more varied the range of ideas in girls, the less room for conceit, presumption and folly. Recreative Education corrects bad temper, produces gentleness, feeds the 'small sweet charities,' and effectually counteracts the chilling apathy of modern fashionable manners.

> Anon., *The Girl's Own Treasury: Specially Designed*
> *for the Amusement and Instruction of Young Ladies*
> (London: Routledge & Sons, 1869), Preface

There are other texts as well, and they are far more contentious. They bring the critical eye of the educated Christian woman to bear upon social and political questions to do with the use and abuse of power in the Church. Here again a double betrayal can be enacted. Either we can reject these voices because no one in the churches really listened and acted on them at the time. In this way we would endorse the opposition of those who failed to listen 'then'. Or we can dismiss them out of hand because these serious and highly articulate Christian women persisted in remaining within the fold. In this way we would endorse the secular judgement which says that religion has nothing to offer women.

This is a highly contemporary question. It exposes something about the hidden voices of history and also about the increasingly silenced voices of our own times.

After all, the educated women who wrote these texts are the foremothers of the feminist theologians of our own times. Once that is understood, it becomes possible to analyse the theological presuppositions we bring to the task of reading what they have to say. A joke? Something maverick? Something irrelevant (because it is 'secular') or redundant (because it is religious)? Or an essential sound in the fully articulated voice of the churches?

The years 1914–1918 marked the final break up of the Victorian era. In the new world which was shaping itself between the two wars it became evident that women's work for the Church could not be effectively performed if it remained solely in the hands of the untrained volunteer. In the first place, the reasonably well educated woman with time on her hands was fast disappearing and, in such places as the new housing areas, was non-existent. The untrained worker, moreover, found herself at a disadvantage in comparison with the professional school teacher, or the trained and experienced social worker in the service of the State. Gone too, was the feudal tradition of respect for social superiors, which had ensured some measure of acceptance for the efforts of even the least experienced. The Church worker found herself taken on her merits, and learned that her usefulness was determined by her own talents, knowledge and power to attract.

Cecilia M. Ady, *The Role of Women in the Church*
(London: The Central Council for Women's Church Work, 1948), p. 15

Women with 'talents, knowledge and power to attract' were the product of education and training. One of the most talented of their number was Kathleen Bliss. She is confident in her certainty when she writes that

Few theologians turn their minds to the enormous work done by women and ask what it all means in terms of a doctrine of the Church. Yet for countless women work for and with women is the only way open to them to make their contribution to the life of the Church. The more vigorous the women's activities in a particular congregation, the more an organisation, group or fellowship tends to become 'the Church' for the woman who finds there Christian fellowship, worship and the upbuilding of her faith. Thus there can arise in practice, although the theory of it is denied, a church within a church, or a church alongside a church. Women constantly feel that in spite of what is said in preaching the men are really 'the Church' and their own participation is derivative from and dependent on, that of men. The question for the future is how the immense achievement of the work of women for women and with women can be made fruitful in the life of the whole Church. This is not a women's question, it is a Church question.

Kathleen Bliss, *The Service and Status of Women in the Churches*
(London: SCM Press Ltd, 1952), pp. 30–1

What Kathleen Bliss saw so clearly in 1952 is still true today. The Christian educators who 'broke the bread of divine knowledge' as and for women, were engaged in a gospel task. So how are we to interpret what they – and the song-women and preachers and social and political activists – did? 'This is not a women's question, it is a Church question.' There is a challenge implied in what Bliss writes. This challenge to our ecclesiology is the abiding legacy of the women who wrote their accounts of the spiritual life; of those who told the story of the missionary endeavours of women; and – supremely – of the women who sought and found a voice with which to say, 'My soul magnifies the Lord.' Where their voice sings out and is clearly heard, it too tells forth a Magnificat for our times.

APPENDIX

~~

Important Dates in the History of the Women's Suffrage Movement

1792 – *Vindication of the Rights of Women* written by Mary Wollstonecraft, which makes a demand for political and economic equality for women.

1818–19 – First Female Reform societies formed as part of the Peterloo agitation for political reform.

1825 – *Appeal of one Half of the Human Race, Women, Against the Pretensions of the Other Half, Men, to Restrain Them in the Political and Thence Civil and Domestic Slavery* by William Thomson, arguing for women's suffrage.

1832 – Reform Bill. For the first time the parliamentary franchise was actually recorded as being limited to men only, because of the insertion of the phrase 'male person'.

1832 – A petition by Miss Mary Smith, a wealthy landowner from Yorkshire, was laid before the House of Commons. Miss Smith argued that if a woman, by the ownership of property, was qualified to vote, then she should have the right to vote.

1837 – First Chartist petition prepared by William Lovett of the London Working Men's Association. This includes female suffrage, but this clause is later dropped. However, in the late 1830s Female Political Associations were formed in various towns and continued to demand an extension of women's rights.

1847 – The first leaflet issued on women's suffrage was published by a Quaker, Ann Knight.

1848 – Female students admitted to London University.

1851 – Ann Knight is involved in starting the Sheffield Association for Female Franchise, which petitions the House of Lords for women's suffrage.

1857 – Matrimonial Causes Act. Women were allowed to sue for divorce on grounds other than adultery. Mothers' rights of access to children after divorce were extended.

1866 – Ladies' Discussion Society organizes Women's Suffrage petition for John Stuart Mill to present to Parliament.

1867 – Representation of the People Bill – a vote to every rate-paying male householder. J. S. Mill moved an amendment to the Bill to substitute the word 'person' for 'man'. He gained 74 votes against 197.

1867 – Society for the Promotion of Women's Suffrage founded by Lydia Becker in Manchester.

1868 – First public meeting to be held in London on the subject of Women's Franchise.

1869 – Municipal Corporations Act: it included an amendment, drafted by Dr Pankhurst, to allow women ratepayers the municipal franchise. Some single women (though no married women) could then vote in local elections.

1870 – First Women's Suffrage Bill drafted by Dr Pankhurst: between 1879 and 1914 there were twenty-eight unsuccessful suffrage bills.

Education Act – women have the right to vote and be elected to the newly created School Boards.

First Married Women's Property Act: allows women to keep what they themselves earned.

1872 – The London School of Medicine for Women opened.

1873 – Custody of Infants Acts: all women could have access to their children if they were separated or divorced.

1874 – Women's Protective and Provident League formed by Emma Parsons to encourage and help women to join trade unions; later changed its name to Women's Trade Union League.

1875 – Emma Paterson and Edith Simcox were the first women delegates to the TUC; they introduced the campaign for equal pay for women workers.

1882 – The Second Married Women's Property Act: this gave women the right to own property and also allowed them to keep some of their earnings.

1884 – Third Reform Act: extends the parliamentary franchise to more adult men – women still excluded. Gladstone put pressure on MPs to defeat the women's suffrage amendment.

1891 – Success of Match-Girls strike led by Annie Besant.

1892 – Rollit's Private Member's Suffrage Bill defeated by only twenty-three votes; this greatly encourage the suffragist organizations, which had become downhearted after the 1884 Act failed to include women in its provision.

1893 – Independent Labour Party formed, which becomes the ideological base for the development of the Labour Party in the 1900s. It is the first political party to give practical support to women's suffrage – although some of the ILP still opposed votes for women.

1893 – Women's Suffrage Societies, inspired by the success of Rollit's Bill, launch a 'Special Appeal' petition – it gets over a quarter of a million women's signatures.

1894 – Married women were given the right to all local franchises and became eligible for election as Parish and District Council- lors and Poor Law Guardians.

1897 – A Private Member's Women's Suffrage Bill passed its second reading by seventy-one votes, but it was talked out and so eventually lost.

1900 – The Manchester-based North of England Society for Women's Suffrage launches its petition among women textile workers in the region.

1903 – Women's Social and Political Union is formed by Mrs Pankhurst at her home in Nelson Street, Manchester. The suffragette organization begins as a small family-based group, but gradually attracts other members of the Manchester Inde- pendent Labour Party.

1905 – Free Trade Hall incident in Manchester: the militant suffragette campaign against the Liberal Party leadership's equivocation on women's suffrage launched. Christabel Pank- hurst and Annie Kennie are imprisoned in Strangeways. The Women's Social and Political Union, the Independent Labour Party and Manchester & Salford Women's Trade and Labour Council organize local protest meetings in support of women's suffrage.

1905 – Bamford Slack's Women's Suffrage Bill is defeated by – once again – being talked out. Feelings among the women present run high, and a protest meeting is held.

1905 – Women's suffrage defeated at the Labour Representation Committee conference in Liverpool. The motion is proposed by an Engineers' delegate and seconded by a working-class woman, Selina Cooper, an ILP delegate from one of Lancashire's textile towns.

1906 – General Election confirms the new Liberal Government, under the leadership of Campbell-Bannerman. The Lancashire & Cheshire Women Textile and other Workers Representation Committee puts up a candidate at Wigan; although he was beaten by the Conservative MP, he came second with over two thousand votes.

Women's Suffrage deputation to Campbell-Bannerman, representing 50,000 women textile workers, 22,000 members of the Women's Co-operative Guild, 1,500 women graduates, 50,000 members of the British Women's Temperance Association, etc. Eight women speak, including Emily Davies, founder of Girton, Mrs Pankhurst for the WSPU, the president of the Women's Co-operative Guild, Sarah Dickenson for the Manchester & Salford Women's Trade and Labour Council, etc. The Prime Minister made no pledges, and could only 'preach the virtue of patience'.

1906 – Marks the growth of the split between the law-abiding suffragettes (co-ordinated within Mrs Fawcett's National Union of Women's Suffrage Societies) and the militant suffragettes, members of the Women's Social and Political Union (WSPU) led by Mrs Pankhurst and Christabel. While the former disagreed that the aim justified the militant means, the WSPU began to escalate its militant campaign against the Liberal Government. They heckled Asquith, the anti-suffrage Chancellor of the Exchequer, and in October Mrs Pankhurst led a raid on Parliament which led to ten arrests, including Annie Kennie and Anne Cobden-Sanderson.

1907 – A women's suffrage resolution seconded by Selina Cooper was defeated at the Labour Party Conference at Belfast.

1907 – Splits develop within the WSPU: Teresa Billington-Grieg and Charlotte Despard oppose the Pankhurst leadership and leave to form the Women's Freedom League.

1907 – Qualification of Women Act: makes women eligible for election to County and Borough Councils and for the Offices of Chair and Mayor (though not yet JPs).

1908 – Anti-suffragist Asquith replaces the more sympathetic Campbell-Bannerman as Prime Minister. The WSPU steps up its militant campaign with window-breaking and stone-throwing.

1909 – WSPU suffragette campaign turns to arson. Hunger strikes and enforced feeding of imprisoned suffragettes begin.

1910 – General Election: Lancashire & Cheshire Women Textile Workers' Representation Committee put up a suffrage candidate in the Rossendale constituency, but he came bottom of the poll with only 693 votes. After the election, with the Liberals still in power, though without a majority, a pro-suffrage all-party Conciliation Committee of fifty-four MPs is set up to draft a women's suffrage bill which would win Conservative party support by restricting the franchise to propertied women. The WSPU calls a truce of its anti-Government militant campaign. But the Bill is defeated as it lacks the vital backing of the government. The WSPU responded with increased lobbying of Parliament, with often-violent clashes between the suffragettes and the police.

1911 – Second Conciliation Bill fails: the WSPU responds with an outbreak of window-breaking.

1912 – Labour Party Conference passes a resolution in favour of adult suffrage but stipulating that Labour MPs must oppose any franchise bill that excludes women. With this welcome support from one of the parliamentary parties, the National

Union of Women's Suffrage Societies, which had previously maintained a line of strict non-party neutrality, sets out to back pro-suffrage Labour candidates at by-elections. To do this it establishes a special Election Fighting Fund and is able to employ over sixty organizations to fight the campaign up and down the country.

1912–14 – The suffragettes within the WSPU escalate their arson campaign in the face of Asquith's and the Liberal's intransigence. Their extreme militancy reached its crescendo when, on Derby Day 1913, Emily Wilding Davison threw herself under the King's horse and was killed: a funeral procession of six thousand accompanied her coffin through the streets of London. With increasing numbers of suffragette prisoners going on hunger strike, and with the government's policy of forced feeding acquiring notoriety, the government responded with the cruel 'Cat and Mouse Act' (Prisoners' Temporary Discharge for Ill-Health Act), which allowed suffragettes to be temporarily discharged to recover their health and then be readmitted to prison.

The WSPU has to go underground to avoid police harassment, and Christabel directs operations from exile in Paris. The WSPU becomes increasingly isolated as both the Pethick-Lawrences and Sylvia Pankhurst find it impossible to condone the WSPU policies. Sylvia Pankhurst helps form the East London Federation of Suffragettes as an alternative to the elitist autocracy of the WSPU; through its paper the *Dreadnought* it campaigned on a wide front, not only for votes for women but also for improving the conditions of home workers, unsupported mothers, etc.

1914 – Outbreak of the First World War: the WSPU suspends its militancy, Christabel Pankhurst returns from Paris, and the suffragettes give their support to the war effort. As more and more men leave, women are recruited in large numbers for munitions work and begin to work in areas from which they have previously been excluded.

1915 – Split within the National Union of Women's Suffrage Societies over the response to the war: all national officers, except Mrs Fawcett and the treasurer, resign as pacifists. With others they helped to form the Women's International League for Peace & Freedom, whose executive included Helena Swanwick, Margaret Ashton, Margaret Bondfield, Mrs Despard, Isabella Ford and Ethel Snowden.

1918 – Representation of the People Act: virtually all men over twenty-one and all women over thirty years are enfranchised.

1919 – Sex Disqualification Removal Act: no one should be disqualified from holding public, civil or judicial posts by their sex or fact of marriage; women are now allowed to be appointed as JPs and sit on the magistrates' bench.

National Union of Women's Suffrage Societies changes its name to the National Union of Societies of Equal Citizenship; Mrs Fawcett retires and Eleanor Rathbone takes over its leadership. Its main effort is specific one-issue campaigns, e.g. divorce law reform, equal guardianship rights for men and women, equal voting rights.

1928 – Equal Franchisement Act: women over twenty-one and under thirty finally given the vote – known as the flapper vote – on the same basis as men.

1969 – Representation of the People Act gave the vote to all men and women over the age of eighteen.

1970 – Equal Pay Act – the Act that said there should be equal pay for equal work.

1975 – Sex Discrimination Act made it illegal to discriminate between men and women in employment, housing, and education.

BIOGRAPHICAL NOTES

~~

CAROLINE ADAMS. The author of *The Prayer Book Pattern*, this eminent Anglican laywoman also wrote about the creed in *Articles of thy Belief*.

CECILIA M. ADY. She wrote *The English Church Today and How it Works* in 1940 and received high praise from the Bishop of Sheffield on the publication of *The Role of Women in the Church*. He wrote of it, 'no book has previously been written showing the part women have played and can play, in the work of the Church for the nation'.

CECIL FRANCES ALEXANDER (1818–95). The prolific writer of a number of fine hymns ('Once in Royal David's City', 'There is a Green Hill', 'All Things Bright and Beautiful', etc.), she was born in Northern Ireland and married the Bishop of Armagh.

ELIZABETH ATKINSON. Staff teacher at the Manchester Municipal Training College of Domestic Economy, where she wrote her *The Teaching of Domestic Science* in 1931.

CLARA LUCAS BALFOUR. Her *Women Worth Emulating* contains studies of Mary Somerville, Charlotte Elliott, Caroline Herschel, Elizabeth Smith, Amelia Opie, Sarah Martin and the Home of the Taylors at Ongar.

DOROTHEA BEALE (1831–1905). She was educated at schools in Paris and London. An educational reformist, she was Principal at Cheltenham Ladies' College from 1858 to 1904.

ELIZABETH MOBERLY BELL. Her history of the rise of the woman doctor was commissioned by the Dean and Governors of the Royal Free Hospital School of Medicine. It focuses on Dr Elizabeth Blackwell, Dr Elizabeth Garrett Anderson and Dr Sophia Jex-Blake.

LUCY A. BENNETT (1850–1927). A British evangelical woman hymn-writer whose work is still published in *Mission Praise*.

KATHLEEN BLISS (1908–89). One-time General Secretary of the Church of England's Board of Education and lecturer in Religious Studies at Sussex University, she was also a well-known broadcaster.

BARBARA LEIGH BODICHON (1827–91). Daughter of Benjamin Smith, a Norwich MP, she married Dr Eugene Bodichon in 1857 and endowed Girton College, Cambridge.

CATHERINE BOOTH (1829–90). Called by God to active ministry in the pulpit, she left the Methodist Church with her husband William. They started the Christian Mission in 1865, a permanent mission to the unconverted, which became known as the Salvation Army in 1878.

JESSIE BOUCHERETT (1825–1905). Called the head and last survivor of an old-established Lincolnshire family' by one biographer, she founded and edited the *Englishwomen's Review* from 1866 to 1871. In 1860 she set up the Society for Promoting the Employment of Women with Barbara Bodichon and Adelaide Anne Procter.

FRANCES MARY BUSS (1827–94). The educational pioneer opened a school in Kentish Town in 1845. She then moved it to Camden Town and subsequently it became North London Collegiate School. She was the contemporary of Dorothea Beale, with whom she had studied at Queen's College in Westminster.

JOSEPHINE BUTLER, née Gray (1828–1906). A lifelong campaigner for women's rights and suffrage, this prominent Anglican laywoman worked for the repeal of the Contagious

Diseases Acts which forced medical examinations upon women in seaports and military towns. A pioneer for women's education, she campaigned on behalf of prostitutes, especially in Liverpool. She married a Canon of Winchester, George Butler.

EDITH CAVELL (1856–1915). She was a governess in Belgium before she returned to Hackney, where she trained as a nurse. In 1907 she became head of nursing at the Birkendael Medical Institute in Brussels and provided an underground support system for French and British soldiers. Court-martialled by the Germans, she was shot and died heroically.

MARY CHAMPNESS. Her study of the hymns in the 1904 version of the Methodist *Hymn Book* was published by Epworth Press.

ELIZABETH JANE CLEPHANE (1830–69). The daughter of the Sheriff Principal of Fife and Kinross, she was a member of the Free Church of Scotland and known as 'Sunbeam' for her good works in Melrose. Her hymns were first published under the title 'Breathings on the Border'.

ALICE CORKRAN. The author of *Meg's Friend, Chapters from the Story of my Girlhood* and *Down the Snow Stairs*, as well as *The Romance of Woman's Influence*.

FANNY CROSBY (1820–1915). Blind from birth, she wrote some nine thousand hymns and gospel songs using a variety of pen-names. This North American evangelical dictated all her work to a scribe. She taught at New York City School for the Blind from 1847 to 1858 and married a blind musician, Alexander Van Alstyne, in 1858.

MARIE CURIE (1867–1934). The French-Polish physicist who discovered radium, polonium and the nature of radioactivity. During World War I she directed radiation therapy services at the Front with a corps of women doctor assistants. She later died of leukaemia. She was the first woman to be a professor at the Sorbonne and the first woman Nobel Prize winner.

EMILY DAVIES (1830–1921). The daughter of John Davies, the Rector of Gateshead, she was prominent in the establishment of Girton College, Cambridge. Her publications included *The Higher Education of Women* in 1866 and *Thoughts on Some Questions Relating to Women* in 1910.

EMILY WILDING DAVISON (1872–1913). Born in Northumberland, she gained a first class honours degree at Oxford in English and became politically active for the cause of suffrage. She died as a result of injuries sustained when she threw herself under the King's horse at the Derby.

LINA ECKENSTEIN. An Anglican scholar and historian.

ELISABETH OF SCHÖNAU (1129–64). She became abbess of the double monastery of Schönau in the diocese of Trier in 1157 and there experienced twelve years of visions and ecstasies which her brother Egbert collated.

SARAH STICKNEY ELLIS (1799–1872). Author of *The Wives of England* (1843) and other books of manners and conduct, she believed in the community of sisterhood but also advocated subservience to men and God.

LEONORA EYLES. The author of *Common Sense about Sex*, she received some 35,000 letters a year and included a chapter on 'Religion and Sublimation' in her *Unmarried but Happy*.

BEATRICE FAIRFAX. The pen-name of Marie Manning, a North American journalist who edited the Women's Page of the *Evening Journal*. Her problem page was, in the eyes of one commentator, 'a daily grist of comedy and pathos into which the columnist put so much heartfelt work, research and common sense'.

MILLICENT FAWCETT (1847–1929). She married the MP Henry Fawcett in 1867 and became active as a suffragist. She wrote *Political Economy for Beginners*, a life of Queen Victoria and other biographies, and a history of the suffrage movement.

ELIZABETH FRY (1780–1845). The great Quaker prison reformer was born near Norwich, one of the seven daughters of John Gurney of Earlham. While her work among prisoners in the UK is well known, it should not be forgotten that she also sought to improve the conditions of convicts being sent to the colonies, and notably women sent to Parramatta in Australia.

JOAN MARY FRY (1826–1955). This Quaker woman gave the Swarthmore Lecture in 1910. She was the founder of the allotment garden scheme and deeply concerned about industrial strife, poverty and unemployment among Welsh miners.

ELIZABETH GARRETT (1838–1917). She qualified to practise medicine through the Society of Apothecaries in 1865 and married J. G. S. Anderson in 1871.

DORA GREENWELL (1821–82). Born into a prosperous Lancashire family which fell upon hard times, she lived with her mother and wrote extensively. A friend of Josephine Butler, she tackled subjects as varied as the treatment of the insane, single women, Lacordaire and the Quaker, John Woolman, as well as writing spirited theological reflections.

ANN GRIFFITHS (1776–95). Born at Dolwar near Llanfyllin, this Welsh farmer's daughter sang her hymns to a servant called Ruth. She repeated these to her husband after Ann's death and he wrote them out.

EMILY MAY GRIMES (1868–1927). An evangelical hymn-writer, she married a man called Crawford, so published under both names before her death in Folkestone.

FRANCES RIDLEY HAVERGAL (1836–79). The youngest of six children, she was reading the Bible at four, and subsequently learned French, German, Welsh, Hebrew and New Testament Greek. She published over thirty collections of hymns, all characterized by strong scriptural and evangelical influences. She was the daughter of the vicar of Astley in Worcester and, as well as writing her own hymns, edited all his music until 1871.

CAROLINE HERSCHEL (1750–1848). She was brought to England from her native Hanover by her brother William, Astronomer Royal. Working as his assistant, she discovered fourteen nebulae and eight comets, and also published two books with the Royal Society. In 1828 she was awarded a Gold Medal by the Royal Astronomical Society and subsequently, at the age of 84, was elected an honorary member along with Mary Somerville.

HILDEGARD OF BINGEN (1098–1179). This German mystic possessed the gift of prophecy even before entering the convent at the age of eight. Here she saw visions and wrote extensively until her death in her eighties. She wrote hymns, poetry, mass settings, medical works and studies of plants and minerals.

CARYLL HOUSELANDER (1901–54). A prolific Roman Catholic spiritual writer of prose and poetry, this laywoman had profound mystical experiences while still in her teens and an acute sense of the presence of Christ in others.

JULIA WARD HOWE (1819–1910). Born in New York, she married the director of the Perkins Institute for the Blind in Boston and worked actively for the abolition of slavery and for women's suffrage.

SOPHIA JEX-BLAKE (1840–1912). The daughter of Thomas Jex-Blake, Proctor of Doctors' Commons, she founded the London School of Medicine for Women in 1874 and gained the right to practise as a doctor in 1877.

ANNIE MARSTON (1852–76). An English evangelical Christian hymn-writer, her work was mainly published in the *Keswick Hymn-Book*.

ELLEN M. McDOUGALL. Late-nineteenth century commentator on hymnody. Her *Songs of the Church* is dedicated to 'our children and grandchildren'. She also wrote *Mothers in Council*, subtitled 'Talks in Mothers' Meetings'.

HANNAH MORE (1745–1833). An Anglican religious writer and philanthropist who set up schools in Somerset and Friendly Societies for the education of girls.

FLORENCE NIGHTINGALE (1820–1910). The English hospital reformer began training as a nurse at Kaiserwerth in 1851. She served as superintendent of a hospital for women in London before taking thirty-eight other nurses off to the Crimea with her in 1854. On her return from Scutari she founded the nursing school at St Thomas's Hospital, London.

PHOEBE PALMER (1807–74). Evangelist and religious author, she was a Methodist and experienced 'entire sanctification' in 1837. She founded the Five Points Mission in New York and conducted holiness revivals all over the USA.

CHRISTABEL PANKHURST (1880–1958). She was born in Manchester and became the leader of the Women's Social and Political Union from 1903 to 1914. After 1920, politics gave way to Christian polemics as she began to preach the second coming.

EMMELINE PETHICK-LAWRENCE (1864–1943). The treasurer of the Women's Social and Political Union from 1906 to 1912, she was joint-editor of *Votes for Women* from 1907 to 1914 and wrote *Does a Man Support his Wife? My Part in a Changing World* in 1938.

EDITH PICTON-TURBERVILLE. Born in 1873, in 1909 she became chairman and head of the Foreign Department at the YWCA. A leading Christian campaigner, she became a Labour Member of Parliament in 1929.

EMMA R. PITMAN. Late-nineteenth century commentator on hymn-writing and on mission history. Her *Lady Missionaries in Foreign Lands* was published in 1913.

ANN PRESTON. Born in Ireland, this Methodist woman moved to Canada and went into service with a Dr Reid and his family. Here she became known as 'Holy Ann' and exercised a ministry of healing and of the word.

EUGENIA PRICE. North American evangelical author of *Woman to Woman*, she broadcast coast to coast and was constantly on the road for the gospel.

ADELAIDE ANNE PROCTER (1825–64). The eldest child of Bryan Waller Procter, she converted to Catholicism in 1851. A hymn-writer and poet, she also wrote under the name Miss Berwick.

CHRISTINA ROSSETTI (1839–94). Poetess and invalid sister of Dante Gabriel Rossetti, she was a high Anglican by temperament and in practice and ended her life as a nun in All Saints' Home, Margaret Street.

MAUDE ROYDEN (1876–1956). Educated at Cheltenham Ladies' College and Lady Margaret Hall, she lectured in the Oxford University extension delegacy and devoted her energies to campaigning for women's suffrage and religious and ethical rights. Unable to preach in the Church of England, she was assistant preacher at the City Temple from 1917 to 1920. During the 1920s and 1930s she travelled in Britain, America, Australia, New Zealand, India and China, campaigning for women and the religious and ethical issues raised by the women's movement.

DOROTHY L. SAYERS (1893–1957). She read modern languages at Somerville College, Oxford, and went on to write detective stories and translate Dante. Her most celebrated work as a Christian apologist was *The Man Born to be King*, the radio play which was broadcast by the BBC in 1941–2.

MARY SOMERVILLE (1780–1872). A scientific writer of distinction, she was the daughter of Sir William Fairfax and married, as her second husband, Sir William Somerville in 1812.

ANNE STEELE (1716–78). A Baptist, she also wrote under the name Theodosia and published 144 hymns, thirty-four versifications of the Psalms and fifty poems on moral subjects.

SARAH GERALDINE STOCK (1838–98). The evangelical author of a number of hymns.

MARY J. STUDLEY. A North American commentator on social mores, her *What Our Girls Ought to Know* was published in 1881.

MARY SUMNER, née Heywood (1829–1921). While studying music in Rome she met George Sumner, married and had three children. He became vicar of Old Alresford in 1851 and she taught the Sunday School and a men's Bible study group. She founded the Mothers' Union and became its first Diocesan and then Central President when it went worldwide. Her vision was that all classes of women could unite in prayer and do God's will by working for their husbands, children, home and country.

EVELYN UNDERHILL (1875–1941). An Anglican laywoman, spiritual director and retreat conductor, she wrote extensively about mysticism and the spiritual life and appears in the liturgical calender of the Episcopal Church as 'mystic and theologian'.

ANNA LETITIA WARING. She published her *Hymns and Meditations* in 1850.

SUSANNAH WESLEY (1669–1742). She married Samuel Wesley in 1689 and raised and educated her children at Epworth.

FRANCES WILLARD (1839–98). An American temperance and suffrage leader, in 1891 she became President of the World Women's Christian Temperance Union and campaigned as a Christian socialist for women's legal rights and better working conditions. She stressed the importance of the family, temperance and the home.

BIBLIOGRAPHY

~

Adams, Caroline, *Articles of Thy Belief* (London: SPCK, 1958).

Ady, Cecilia M., *The Role of Women in the Church* (The Central Council for Women's Church Work, 1948).

Anon., *The Girl's Own Treasury: Specially Designed for the Amusement and Instruction of Young Ladies* (London: Routledge & Sons, 1869).

Atkinson, Elizabeth, *The Teaching of Domestic Science* (London: Methuen & Co. Ltd, 1931).

Balfour, Clara Lucas, *Women Worth Emulating* (London: Sunday School Union, 1907).

Bell, E. Moberly, *Storming the Citadel: The Rise of the Woman Doctor* (London: Constable & Co. Ltd, 1953).

Bingham, Helen E., *An Irish Saint* (London: Morgan & Scott Ltd, n.d.).

Bliss, Kathleen, *The Service and Status of Women in the Churches* (London: SCM Press Ltd, 1952).

Booth, Catherine, *Papers of Practical Religion* (London: Salvation Army Book Stores, n.d.).

Booth-Tucker, F. de L., *The Life of Catherine Booth: The Mother of the Salvation Army*, vol. 2 (London: The Salvation Army, 1891).

Champness, Mary, *Half Hours with the Hymn Book* (London: Charles H. Kelley, n.d.).

Chappell, Jennie, *Women of Worth* (London: S. W. Partridge & Co. Ltd, n.d.).

Church Praise (London: James Nisbet & Co. Ltd, 1907).

Cochrane, Jeanie Douglas, *Peerless Women* (London: Collins, n.d.).

Corkran, Alice, *The Romance of Woman's Influence* (London: Blackie & Son Ltd, n.d.).

Curie, Eve, *Madame Curie* (London: Heinemann, 1938).

Eckenstein, Lina, *The Women of Early Christianity* (London: The Faith Press, 1935).

Ellis, Mrs, *The Mothers of Great Men* (Edinburgh: W. P. Nimmo, Hay & Mitchell, 1902).

Emily, Sister, *Was Eve Guilty?* (London: Messrs Hill, Cook & Lane, n.d.).

Eva of Friedenshort, Sister, *The Working of the Holy Spirit in Daily Life* (London: Hodder & Stoughton, 1933).

Eyles, Leonora, *Careers for Women* (London: Elkin Mathews & Marrot, 1930).

Eyles, Leonora, *Unmarried but Happy* (London: Victor Gollancz Ltd, 1947).

Fairfax, Beatrice, *Ladies, Now and Then* (London: John Gifford Ltd, 1944).

Fawcett, Millicent G. and Turner, E. M., *Josephine Butler* (London: The Association for Moral and Social Hygiene, 1927).

Field, Mrs E. M., *Addresses to Mothers* (London: James Clarke & Co. Ltd, 1926).

Fletcher, Sheila, *Maude Royden* (Oxford: Basil Blackwell, 1991).

Fry, Joan Mary, *The Communion of Life* (London: Headley Brothers, 1910).

Fulford, Roger, *Votes for Women* (London: Faber & Faber, 1958).

Greenwell, Dora, *Covenant of Life and Peace* (London: H. R. Allenson Ltd, n.d.).

Greenwell, Dora, *The Patience of Hope* (London: Gibbings & Co., 1894).

Greenwell, Dora, *Two Friends* (London: The Epworth Press, 1952).

Havergal, Frances Ridley, *The Ministry of Song* (London: James Nisbet & Co., 1885)

Hensley, Almon, *Love and the Woman of Tomorrow* (London: Drane's, 1913).

Holmes, E. E., *In Watchings Often* (London: Longman, Green & Co., 1912).

Hopkins, Ellice, *The Power of Womanhood; or, Mothers and Sons* (London: Wells Gardner, Darton & Co., 1899).

Hopkins, Mrs Evan, *Hymns of Consecration and Faith* (London: Marshall Brothers Ltd, n.d.).

Horth, Lillian B. and Arthur C., *101 Things for Girls to Do: Being a Review of Simple Crafts and Household Subjects* (London: B. T. Batsford Ltd, 1932).

Huvelin, Abbé, *Addresses to Women* (London: Burns & Oates, 1936).

James, John Angell, *Female Piety or the Young Woman's Friend and Guide through Life to Immortality* (London: Hamilton Adams & Co., 1877).

Kamm, Josephine, *How Different from Us: A Biography of Miss Buss and Miss Beale* (London: The Bodley Head, 1958).

Kamm, Josephine, *Rapiers and Battleaxes* (London: George Allen & Unwin Ltd, 1966).

Legget, Jane, *Local Heroines: A Women's History Gazetteer to England, Scotland and Wales* (London: Pandora Press, 1988).

McDougall, Lady Ellen M., *Songs of the Church with Stories of their Writers* (London: Charles H. Kelly, n.d.).

More, Hannah, *The Letters of Hannah More* (London: The Bodley Head Ltd, 1925).

More, Hannah, *Strictures on the Modern System of Female Education*, vol. 1 (London: T. Cadell Jun. and W. Davies, 1801).

Newcomb, H., *The Young Lady's Guide to the Harmonious Development of Christian Character* (London: T. Nelson & Sons, 1854).

Newsholme, Arthur, *Hygiene: A Manual of Personal and Public Health* (London: George Gill & Sons, 1892).

Pankhurst, Christabel, *The Lord Cometh* (London: Morgan & Scott, 1923).

Pankhurst, Christabel, *Pressing Problems of the Closing Age* (London: Morgan & Scott Ltd, 1924).

Pankhurst, Christabel, *The World's Unrest: Vision of the Dawn* (London: Morgan & Scott Ltd, n.d.).

Parker, Olive, *For the Family's Sake* (London: Mowbray's, 1975).

Picton-Turberville, Edith, *Christ and Woman's Power* (London: Morgan & Scott Ltd, 1919).

Picton-Turberville, Edith, *Life is Good* (London: Frederick Muller Ltd, 1939).

Pitman, Mrs E. R., *Lady Hymn Writers* (London: T. Nelson & Sons, 1892).

Price, Eugenia, *Woman to Woman* (Grand Rapids: Zondervan, 1959).

Price, Mary and Glenday, Nonita, *Reluctant Revolutionaries: A Century of Headmistresses 1874–1974* (London: Pitman Publishing, 1974).

Raven, Charles E., *Women and Holy Orders: A Plea to the Church of England* (London: Hodder & Stoughton Ltd, 1928).

Redemption Hymnal (Eastbourne: Victory Press, 1951).

Rizk, Helen Salem, *Stories of the Christian Hymns* (London: Hodder & Stoughton, 1964).

Rossetti, Christina G., *Verses* (London: SPCK, 1898).

Routley, Erik, *Hymns and Human Life* (London: John Murray, 1952).

Royden, A. Maude, *Blessed Joan of Arc* (London: Sidgwick & Jackson, Ltd, 1923).

Royden, A. Maude, *Christ Triumphant* (London: G. P. Putnam's Sons, 1924).

Royden, A. Maude, *The Friendship of God* (London: G. P. Putnam's Sons, 1924).

Royden, A. Maude, *Here and Hereafter* (London: Putnam, 1933).

Royden, A. Maude, *The Making of Women* (London: George Allen & Unwin Ltd, 1917).

Royden, A. Maude, *Political Christianity* (London: G. P. Putnam's Sons, 1922).

Royden, A. Maude, *Women at the World's Crossroads* (New York: The Woman's Press, 1922).

Royden, A. Maude, *Women's Partnership in the New World* (London: George Allen & Unwin Ltd, 1941).

Ryder, Rowland, *Edith Cavell* (London: Book Club Edition, 1975).

Sayers, Dorothy L., *Creed or Chaos?* (London: Methuen & Co. Ltd, 1947).

Silvester, James, *Hannah More: Christian Philanthropist* (London: Thynne & Co., Ltd, 1934).

Smith, G. Barnett, *Noble Womanhood: A Series of Biographical Sketches* (London: SPCK, 1898).

Strachey, Ray, *The Cause: A Short History of the Women's Movement in Great Britain* (London: G. Bell & Sons Ltd, 1928).

Stuart, Dorothy Margaret, *The Girl Through the Ages* (London: George G. Harrap & Co. Ltd, 1933).

Studley, Mary J., *What Our Girls Ought to Know* (New York: Holbrook & Co., 1881).

Sumner, Mrs, *Home Life* (London: Wells Gardner, Darton & Co., n.d.).

Talmage, T. DeWitt, *Marriage and Home Life* (Edinburgh: Oliphant, Anderson & Ferrier, 1886).

Taylor, Gordon, *Companion to the Song Book of the Salvation Army* (London: Salvation Army, 1989).

Todd, Janet, (ed.), *Dictionary of British Women Writers* (London: Routledge, 1989).

Trustees of the Keswick Convention, *The Keswick Hymn-Book* (London: Marshall, Morgan & Scott Ltd, n.d.).

Uglow, Jennifer, (ed.), *The Macmillan Dictionary of Women's Biography* (London: The Macmillan Press, 1989).

Underhill, Evelyn, *The School of Charity* (London: Longmans, Green & Co., 1934).

Vincent, Charles and Wood, D. J., *The Hymnal Companion to the Book of Common Prayer* (London: Longmans, Green & Co., 1922).

Wallace, Carlton, (ed.), *The Housewife's Pocket Book* (London: Evans Brothers Ltd, 1953).

Ward, Maisie, *Caryll Houselander: That Divine Eccentric* (London: Sheed & Ward, 1962).

Watt, Margaret H., *The History of the Parson's Wife* (London: Faber & Faber Ltd, 1943).

Willard, Frances E., *Woman in the Pulpit* (Boston: D. Lothrop Co., 1888).

Wintle, W. J. and Witts, Florence, *Florence Nightingale and Frances E. Willard: The Story of Their Lives* (London: Sunday School Union, n.d.).

Wise, Daniel, *The Young Man's Counsellor: or Sketches and Illustrations of the Duties and Dangers of Young Men* (London: Yorkshire J. S. Publishing and Stationery Co. Ltd, n.d.).

Wood, Mrs G. R. Harding, *Women – Are You Listening?* (London: Lutterworth Press, 1954).

INDEX

~~

Adams, Caroline 89–90
Ady, Cecilia M. 73–4, 105–6, 153–4
A. J. R. 116
Alexander, Cecil Frances 31–2
Anthony, Susan B. 123
Atkinson, Elizabeth 71–3, 150–51

Balfour, Clara Lucas 143–7
Beale, Dorothea 104, 107–8, 113, 127–8, 139
Bell, Elizabeth Moberly 75–6, 97
Bennett, Lucy A. 10–11, 28–9
Bingham, Helen E. 50
Bliss, Kathleen 67–8, 88–9, 154
Bodichon, Barbara Leigh 113
Booth, Catherine 45–6, 64–5
Booth-Tucker, F. de L. 46–7
Boucerett, Jessie 113
Buss, Frances Mary 104, 107–8, 113, 127
Butler, Josephine 86–8

Cavell, Edith 94–5
Champness, Mary 25
Chappell, Jennie 137–8
Cobbe, Frances 137–8
Corkran, Alice 145–6
Craig, Isa 113
Crosby, Fanny 11–12
Curie, Eve 148
Curie, Marie 148

Davies, Emily 113, 127
Davison, Emily Wilding 121–2
DeWitt Talmage, T. 66, 69

Eckenstein, Lina 101–3
Ellis, Sarah Stickney 43–4
Emily, Sister 101 106–7
Eva of Friedenshort, Sister 53
Eyles, Leonora 54–5, 74, 80–81, 108–9, 140

Fairfax, Beatrix 123–4
Fawcett, Millicent 86–8
Field, E. M. 84–5
Fry, Elizabeth 32–3
Fry, Joan Mary 60
Fulford, Roger 120–22

Garrett, Elizabeth 113
Glenday, Nonita 136
Greenwell, Dora 52, 62, 74–5
Griffiths, Ann 16–18
Grimes, Emily May 21, 35, 36

Havergal, Frances Ridley 13–14
Hensley, Almon 117
Herschel, Caroline 145–7
Hilda, Saint 104
Holmes, E. E. 95–6
Hopkins, Ellice 106
Horth, Lillian B. and Arthur C. 83–4
Houselander, Caryll 91–3
Howey, Elsie 120
Huvelin, Abbe 109

James, John Angell 44–5
Jex-Blake, Sophia 113

Kamm, Josephine 104, 107–8, 113, 139

McDougall, Ellen M. 30–31
Marston, Annie 19–20
Mill, John Stuart 113
More, Hannah 132–5, 138

Newcomb, H. 47, 48, 55–6, 72
Newsholme, Arthur 57
Nightingale, Florence 98–100, 143

Palmer, Phoebe 39
Pankhurst, Christabel 48, 125–6
Parkes, Bessie Rayner 113
Pethick-Lawrence, Emmeline 120
Picton-Turbervill, Edith 118–19, 124–5
Pitman, Emma 12–14, 16, 32–4
Preston, Ann 50
Price, Eugenia 56–7
Price, Mary 136

Raven, Charles E. 110–12
Rossetti, Christina 23
Routley, Eric 15
Royden, Maude 58–9, 65, 70, 80, 81–2, 93, 108, 120–21, 147–8

Sayers, Dorothy L. 61–2, 90
Stock, Sarah Geraldine 23–5
Somerville, Mary 143–5
Stanton, Elizabeth Cady 123
Steele, Anne 27
Stone, Lucy 123
Strachey, Ray 122
Stuart, Dorothy Margaret 131–2, 136–7
Studley, Mary J. 83, 149–52
Sumner, Mary 69–70

Underhill, Evelyn 68–9

Wallace, Carlton 77–9
Ward, Maisie 92–3
Watt, Margaret H. 129–31
Wesley, Susannah 43–4, 129–31
Willard, Frances 37, 39–42, 44, 117–18, 141
Wintle, W. J. 85, 91, 98–100, 117–18, 141, 143
Wise, Daniel 100–101
Witts, Florence 85, 91, 98–100, 117–18, 141, 143
Wood, G. R. Harding 83